CO-023

A COMPLETE INTRODUCTION TO

SNAKES

COMPLETELY ILLUSTRATED IN FULL COLOR

The spectacular colors of this milk snake, Lampropeltis triangulum, *have made it a very popular species with advanced hobbyists.*

A freshly molted snake shows its most beautiful colors. Cream becomes yellow or white, gray becomes black or shiny brown, rusts become brilliant reds.

A COMPLETE INTRODUCTION TO

SNAKES

COMPLETELY ILLUSTRATED IN FULL COLOR

The vivid yellows of this young New Guinea tree python will turn to green as it matures. Although spectacular, rare and expensive specimens such as this are not for the beginning snake keeper. Chondropython viridis. Photo by B. Kahl.

Mervin F. Roberts

Distributed in the UNITED STATES by T.F.H. Publications, Inc., 211 West Sylvania
Avenue, Neptune City, NJ 07753; in CANADA to the Pet Trade by H & L Pet Sup-
plies Inc., 27 Kingston Crescent, Kitchener, Ontario N2B 2T6; Rolf C. Hagen Ltd.,
3225 Sartelon Street, Montreal 382 Quebec; in CANADA to the Book Trade by
Macmillan of Canada (A Division of Canada Publishing Corporation), 164 Com-
mander Boulevard, Agincourt, Ontario M1S 3C7; in ENGLAND by T.F.H. Publica-
tions Limited, 4 Kier Park, Ascot, Berkshire SL5 7DS; in AUSTRALIA AND THE
SOUTH PACIFIC by T.F.H. (Australia) Pty. Ltd., Box 149, Brookvale 2100 N.S.W.,
Australia; in NEW ZEALAND by Ross Haines & Son, Ltd., 18 Monmouth Street,
Grey Lynn, Auckland 2 New Zealand; in SINGAPORE AND MALAYSIA by MPH
Distributors (S) Pte., Ltd., 601 Sims Drive, #03/07/21, Singapore 1438; in the
PHILIPPINES by Bio-Research, 5 Lippay Street, San Lorenzo Village, Makati Rizal;
in SOUTH AFRICA by Multipet Pty. Ltd., 30 Turners Avenue, Durban 4001. Pub-
lished by T.F.H. Publications Inc. Manufactured in the United States of America
by T.F.H. Publications, Inc.

Contents

Introduction

This is a book for people who have just begun to take an interest in snakes; it is an introduction. Here you will find something about snakes' place in the Tree of Life, their anatomy, venoms, diet, habits, requirements when in captivity, and desirability as pets. A complete library of snake literature could easily fill a large room.

The natural color photographs are among the best in the world. They were selected to show you snakes in the wide range of colors, forms, and sizes presently available to pet keepers. A few venomous species are included only for purposes of comparison. No reader of this book has any business owning or handling any venomous snake. If you want to play Russian roulette, do it with drugs or alcohol in automobiles or by skating on thin ice. Snake keepers have enough problems without having unnecessary bad publicity thrust upon them.

This is my third T.F.H. book about snakes in these past 30 years. I have had plenty of time to think about what a beginner needs to know, wants to know, and doesn't know but thinks he knows. I've also had plenty of time to discover how little most of us (myself included) know with certainty about these fascinating animals.

As with previous books, I have been aided by Dr. Richard G. Zweifel, Curator, Department of Herpetology, American Museum of Natural History, New York; Dr. Robert S. Clark, a veterinarian with a practice in Old Lyme; Mr. John Dommers, Director of the N. E. Regional Office of The Humane Society of the United States; Mr. William Haast, Director of Miami Serpentarium Labs., Salt Lake City; Mr. Louis W. Porras, proprietor of Zooherp in Sandy, Utah; Dr. Arthur English of Old Lyme; and my loyal wife Edith, who types from handwritten manuscripts that even I sometimes have trouble reading. Surely a few mistakes slipped in; please don't blame these people; I had the last word.

Mervin Roberts
Old Lyme, Connecticut

Garter snakes and ribbon snakes have long been the average beginner's first snakes. This fine ribbon snake, Thamnophis proximus, *could have a long captive life and might even breed if properly kept. Photo by B. Kahl.*

What Have We Here?

Our culture is so full of references and allusions to snakes that when someone wants to keep a few as pets there will surely be someone else who lifts an eyebrow or makes a wisecrack or, worse still, makes a dogmatic but inaccurate statement—remarks such as "They are so slimy," "What if it should bite you?," "I dread the thought of having one choke me," "Why would a 'normal' person want one of *them*?," "Don't you have something better to do with your time?".

You might try any one of these responses:

"The Chinese consider them to be a culinary delicacy—better even than dog."

"No one in Hoboken, New Jersey, has ever been suffocated by a snake (but many years ago an exotic dancer in Union City, N.J., did have a run-in with a policeman who said that her boa didn't cover enough of her when she danced with it)."

"Snakes are clean, quiet, long-lived, odorless, and inexpensive to feed. Also, they don't harbor fleas and they don't irritate people with feather or hair allergies."

"Snakes are graceful and interesting; a house is not a home without a snake."

"A cow barn without a milk snake is like a kiss without a squeeze."

The delicate beauty of albino snakes makes them very desirable. This is a Thamnophis butleri. *Photo by J. Gee.*

All of us seem to know what a snake is, but by way of a review we might remind ourselves of the following:

All snakes are reptiles. Every snake has one or two lungs, but no snake has gills. They have scales but no slime. They eat animals, but not vegetables. They have between 100 and 400 vertebrae. They do not tear or cut their food, but eat the whole thing. The lower jaws of a snake are loosely attached to each other. Snakes have no external ears or even ear openings. Most have eyes, but none have movable eyelids. Some snakes

The basic cage for a small terrestrial snake—an old aquarium, a simple substrate, a rock, a bit of greenery, and a cover.

are very, very poisonous, some are non-poisonous, and some are in-between. It would be more appropriate to use the word "venomous" than "poisonous" since the toxic substance produced by snakes is properly called venom.

Some female snakes lay eggs and some give birth to living young.

Some snakes have two little spurs near the base of the tail that represent vestigial remnants of legs. The ancestors of snakes, millions of years ago, according to the fossil record, did have legs.

Snakes are generally considered to be "cold blooded," but some species do have a bit of control over their temperature.

When a snake sheds, only a very thin dead outer layer of skin comes off.

Snakes are found on every continent except Antarctica and in the water as well as on land. Some spend most of their time in trees and others are often underground for long periods. There are no native snakes in

Ireland, Iceland, or New Zealand. Why it was a serpent who got Eve into trouble with the apple is something I never understood.

Some snakes are rare, endangered, and protected by law; others are legal to own but are terribly expensive; some are dangerous and should not be kept captive by pet owners, however knowledgeable, because of the risk to others. Fortunately, there are also a great number of safe, legal, inexpensive, interesting, hardy, long-lived species that make fascinating pets. This experience in snake keeping will be your opportunity to find out how tolerant, really tolerant, your family can be. Or maybe you will find them to be narrow-minded, biased, ignorant, and unimaginative. Some folks are that way.

In 1956, the most accurate number we had for all the species and subspecies of snakes north of Mexico was 265. In 1978 that number was 276, and in the most current list it is 264. These numbers will surely continue to change a bit from time to time. That doesn't mean we are witnessing new creation or evolution or extinction or even discovery. Another number may be just another arrangement as still another scientist takes still another look at these reptiles.

The Pet Snake

Choosing a Pet Snake

Please bear in mind: If you want an animal that will follow you around the house and jump with joy whenever you come home or open the refrigerator, get yourself a dog. If you still want to keep a snake, here are a few firm rules for a beginner.

1: *Choose a snake whose size you can afford to house.* It would be nice if the diagonal measure of the cage could be at least equal the length of the snake. This becomes difficult if you have a 6-foot specimen, but at least you should provide enough room for the animal to arrange and rearrange its coils without becoming jammed. There should be room in the cage for water for drinking and for occasional bathing. If a warming light or heater is provided, then also a shaded or cool area must be available.

2: *Choose a non-venomous species.* Perhaps you think you are dexterous enough to handle any snake, but there is always the one time when an ignorant or unauthorized person gets into the wrong cage. If you want to risk your own life, I cannot either prevent you or encourage you, but if you knowingly endanger someone else, then what you are doing is criminal.

3: *Choose for your first pet snake an inexpensive and hardy species.* There are plenty—so many that you can even pick a color if you wish—choose green, blue, brown, black, pink or checkered or banded or striped. For less than a day's pay you can probably get what you want.

4: *Pick a snake you can afford to house properly.* The cage should be professionally constructed to assure security. You must keep the snake in and you must keep other animals and people out. The inside of the cage must be smooth and easy to clean. There must be adequate ventilation. More about cages later.

5: *Choose a specimen that you know is eating regularly and that you know you can properly feed.* Ask for a demonstration *before* you put down any money.

Arboreal snakes require a higher cage so climbing branches can be put in.

6: *Choose a size and a color that appeal to you*—something you won't get tired of. Your snake could easily live a long time.

7: *Choose a healthy, well-fed specimen.* Shun any that are deformed, lumpy, limp, or skinny. Twenty years from now, when you become expert or at least knowledgeable, you might take on a hospital case and nurse it back to health, but for starters, start batting with no strikes already against you. For example, don't

11

begin with a snake whose eyes are clouded over—it is about to molt. Often such an animal is mean and prone to bite; also it may not want to eat until after it sheds, and it may have trouble shedding. For the first go-around, let that be a problem for someone else. For another example, sometimes freshly caught snakes are infested with mites or ticks. These can be removed and eliminated by experienced snake keepers. Later I will tell you how.

8: *Avoid species that spend their lives underground.* You will want to see your pet. Avoid species that are known to be nocturnal—for the same reason. Choose a species that naturally spends most of its time on dry land or in trees. Wet cages or aquariums require special skills on your part or they will quickly become smelly and unhealthful.

9: *If you are getting started, get started slowly.* Start with just one snake. There is a lot to learn about snake keeping, and much depends on experience that cannot come from a book. Experience comes from experience. Patiently observe and then digest what you have observed. Only then will what you see make sense. For example, a coiled snake may be about to

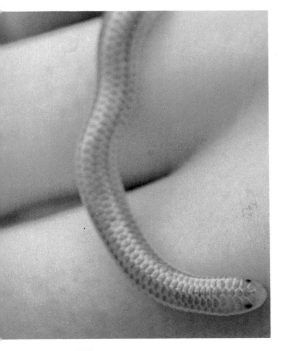

Left: Leptotyphlops humilis, *a burrower that once put in the cage will never be seen again. Photo by K. Lucas, Steinhart Aqu.* Above: *Boa constrictors make good pets for hobbyists who have gotten beyond the "first snake" phase.* Boa constrictor. *Photo by P. J. Stafford.*

strike or it may be coiled because it is cold or perhaps it is coiled because it is relaxed and busy digesting a recent meal. With experience you will be able to recognize those subtle differences in appearance that make all the difference. Have a little humility as you get started with snakes. It can be fascinating fun.

Garter snakes are relatively inexpensive, easy to obtain, feed well in captivity, give birth readily, and tame easily. Photo by B. Kahl.

Handling Snakes

Treat every snake with humane and thoughtful care, but that doesn't mean that you need to lavish affection on it. Sweet words will avail you nothing; it is virtually deaf. What you should do after properly caging and feeding it is to treat the snake gently but firmly so that it, in turn, will become docile. Granted, some species (such as bull snakes) are easier to tame than others (such as water snakes), and some individuals will be more tractable than others, but all that not withstanding, any animal will be better with firm, consistent, and humane care.

When you enter a room where a snake is caged, don't slam the door or bang on the cage. Avoid flashing a light if your snake is in

13

the dark. Snakes don't have eyelids to close, but they do seem to rest or sleep from time to time.

When you want to hold a snake, you might be wise to let it come to you rather than to reach into its cage. That cage is the snake's home. He may wish to defend it.

When you grasp a snake, try for a firm, gentle grasp immediately behind its head. Depending on how heavy or long it is, you should support its body

not wear gloves, however.

If you are in the Great Outdoors on a snake hunt, you might start by assuring yourself that there are no venomous snakes in the area. Even a copperhead (which probably could not kill you) would be able to kill your dog or worse, your father's dog. Carry a burlap sack and a stick which has a 90° turn or a fork or a "T" at the end. Call it a snake stick and use it to pin the animal to the ground while

Collecting your own specimens has some advantages if it can be done without legal problems. Even if you find no keepable snakes, you might stumble across other interesting things, such as a mating "dance" by male copperheads.

somewhere with your other hand. If the snake drapes itself over your arm, so much the better. Never lift any snake by its tail. Some snakes would prefer to lose part of their tail than to be lifted that way. If a tail is broken off, it may grow back somewhat, but it will never be as long and smoothly tapered as the original.

Should you wear gloves when handling a non-venomous snake? Yes, if the snake is known to be or believed to be nippy. Most experienced snake keepers do

you assure yourself that it is non-venomous and that you really want to keep it. In most rural areas of the U.S. and many suburban areas as well, there are more snakes available to be captured than all the fanciers in the country could possibly want.

If you have a captive snake in summertime that is native to your area but fear that you will not be able to provide food for it in winter, release it early enough in autumn so it can have time to find a proper place to hibernate.

Never release an exotic snake. It will either die or it will upset the ecosystem. If you have a snake that isn't a local native and you wish to dispose of it, contact your nearest zoo, college zoology department, or pet shop dealer.

Never hunt snakes until you find out from an official source how to comply with the law. Many species of snakes are strictly protected in many places. Your state's Department of Conservation or Environmental Protection or Fish and Game or equivalent department will either inform you or arrest you—your choice. Many states also have laws about what species you can legally possess and may even require that you purchase an inexpensive hobbyist's permit. Some cities also have laws, especially about keeping large pythons and venomous species.

If you encounter a snake so badly diseased or injured that it cannot be saved, one humane and inexpensive method of killing it is by placing it in a cloth bag and putting it in a freezer. The snake will become numb, its senses will be quickly and painlessly wiped out, and when the animal is totally as hard as an ice cube, it will also be as dead as a door nail. A large snake might require several days before it is thoroughly frozen, although it will be insensible within an hour. You might also store a dead specimen this way for future examination if the circumstances of its death are of special interest.

In many parts of the country various species of snakes are protected by law. Collecting Mexican kingsnakes, Lampropeltis mexicana, is a no-no in Texas. Photo by R. W. Applegate.

Safety

If you should visit someone who has a large snake, let's say a specimen that is at least as thick as your wrist, you may notice that there is a large mirror in the room where the snake is kept. The reason is for safety. If the snake should drape itself around a person, there might be a problem of disentanglement. If you cannot find an end of a long snake you could have trouble unwinding it. The mirror is the insurance policy.

Another insurance policy for snake keepers is a locked door.

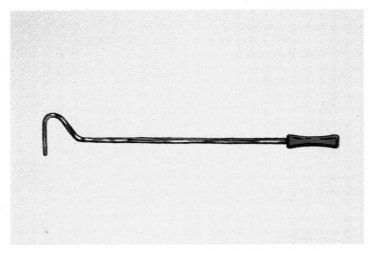

Some type of snake stick is essential if you plan on collecting snakes or on handling specimens over a few feet long, even if they are harmless. Of course venomous species must be handled—if at all—only with a snake stick.

This is good for the snakes, which might be molested by unthinking people or animals. It is also a second cage door against the time when the actual door is inadvertently left open or whatever. If you have the attitude that any problem is the fault of the snake or another person, then you have no business keeping snakes or any other potentially dangerous or frightening animals.

You and your perfectly harmless snake can cause as much harm to another person through a fright as through a bite. Don't assume that because you are not afraid of your pet that all other people will be likewise. It just isn't so and it never will be. You should handle and display your snake as though it is dangerous and avoid all risks. Really, it doesn't matter whether the snake bites someone or just frightens that person down a

flight of stairs or through a window or over a piece of furniture. The cause and effect are the same.

A tame and usually gentle pet snake will sometimes become mean just before it is about to

molt. The old skin often becomes cloudy over the eyes, and as the snake loses some of its vision its personality may change. Provide your pet with an opportunity to take a bath. This may help it to shed. *Don't peel the skin!* Just provide the snake with something in the cage to rub against; a branch of a tree with the bark on, perhaps. Let the snake pull off its own dead skin by itself when *it* is ready.

Transportation of Snakes

They need air at the same pressure that you and I need it. They need warmth—a chill could hurt any snake and a freezing

Molting   an activity in which every snake must participate at least one or two times a year. Lampropeltis getulus. *Photo by K. Lucas, Steinhart Aqu.*

temperature would likely kill just about any snake. Some species are more hardy than others, but eventually all will succumb.

If you want to ship a snake by public carrier, you will quickly discover that there are all sorts of rules and regulations to discourage you.

I don't recommend that you sedate a snake in order to make shipping easier. It is too easy to overdo the treatment and create a zombie.

Bag your specimen in a strong, porous cloth bag (a sturdy pillowcase is the old standby). Make it as roomy as necessary to permit the animal to coil and recoil into different positions. Tie the mouth of the bag with two separate and independent cords. Do not include any food or fluids. A snake will do quite nicely for a few days without eating or drinking. They do it all the time.

Pack the bag in a styrofoam box that is perforated to permit air to circulate. A few half-inch diameter holes should suffice. The bag should fit into the box closely enough so the animal doesn't get knocked about when the baggage is moved. The styrofoam box should be taped and/or strapped. Labels should be firmly affixed both inside— perhaps tied to the bag—and also on the outside. This advice might not be in exact conformity with what the trucker or bus line or airline might require. To comply with the law, you must do exactly what the carrier tells you. It is illegal to ship snakes by mail.

When people travel with their pet snakes, they generally put them in a dog or cat shipping container and cover the openings with opaque fabric. The problem will not be with the animal but with the busybodies.

Caution: Many airplane cargo

Small dog or cat carriers are fine for carrying snakes, if the snakes are securely bagged.

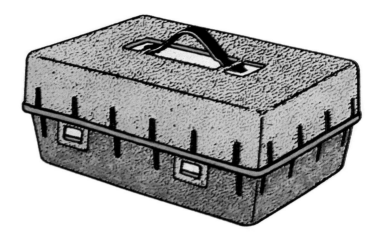

compartments are not heated and/or not pressurized. If a snake is to be moved by aircraft, you should look into this *before* you get to the airport.

Anatomy of Snakes

The bones of a snake's jaws are strongly connected but not closely linked. This makes it possible for a snake to swallow an animal that is wider than its head. When a snake eats, it will grasp its meal with the incurved teeth of those loosely linked four jaws, i.e., the upper and lower, right and left (plus most snakes have additional rows of secondary teeth in the upper mouth). With both left jaws holding, it will disengage the lower jaw right hand connection and take a new bite farther forward. When the right hand jaws are in position and those teeth are engaged, the teeth of the lower left jaw will be disconnected, advanced, and reconnected. All snakes of all sizes eat that way, regardless of whether they are venomous or non-venomous or slightly venomous. This description is not absolutely precise, but it should suffice until you become an expert.

If a snake is venomous it may or may not be furnished with a pair of fangs in the forward ends of the upper jaws that serve to inject poison into the wounds they create. Some venomous snakes don't have such a pair of hollow fangs (these may be likened to hypodermic needles), but rather they may have grooved fangs or they may have no fangs in front but instead there will be long sharp grooved rear teeth. In a few snakes regular teeth may create a wound into which the venom will seep, but this is very exceptional.

A staged fight between a mongoose and a cobra. The mongoose will almost always win.

Snake teeth are relatively long, curved and thin. Often they will break or be pulled out. This is no great inconvenience for a snake since new teeth or fangs will grow back quickly to replace those that are lost. If you are bitten, you will find that each of many teeth must be dislodged before you can separate yourself from your attacker. By pushing the head of the snake forward, you will disengage with less damage than if you should pull it away. Broken teeth in captive animals often lead to serious infections in the snake's mouth, so it is better for your snake's health not to let it bite you.

Some of the dreaded cobras are able to spit venom considerable distances. They are reputed to be able to aim at the eyes of an enemy. This might be part of a defense by a snake against a mongoose, that legendary mink-like creature made famous by Rudyard Kipling in one of his stories. Usually, in such an encounter the mongoose wins and eats the snake.

Spurs, a pair at the base of the tail on some boa constrictors, pythons, and other primitive forms, are believed to be relics of

Detail of the anal spur of a boa. These are the snake's only external remnant of legs. Photo by J. Dodd.

evolution. Best evidence suggests that snakes developed, over eons, from lizard-like reptiles that had legs. Therefore systematists (these are scientists who attempt to arrange forms of life into related groups) consider the pythons and boas as among the most primitive or ancient of the snakes. Today, male snakes of some species which have spurs will use them to caress their mates while they are entwined.

Since many snakes burrow in sand, any opening or moist surface on the body would be a trap for irritating particles. Mother Nature has handled this problem quite nicely for snakes. Their eyes are completely covered with a lens of dry transparent skin (called a spectacle) that peels off with the rest of the skin when the animal molts.

There is not only no outer ear flap, there is no ear opening, and for all intents and purposes there is practically no ear. Can snakes hear? Not much. How about the snake charmer and his flute? Well, it seems that snakes sway to the music because they are watching and following the swaying movement of the musician and not the sound of his instrument. Were the cobras used by the Indian snake charmer rendered non-venomous? Probably not; even if the fangs are removed they will be replaced, and the poison will still be available for spitting and

The smooth, tightly placed head scales of this burrowing boa, Calabaria reinhardti, *and its small eye are adaptations for a life underground. Photo by P. J. Stafford.*

chewing. So what keeps the snake charmer alive? My answer is illogically unassailable. Did you ever know of a dead snake charmer? Of course not. If you ever see a swaying cobra coming out of the basket to the tune of flute music, you will notice that the snake charmer is very much alive. If he were dead, he wouldn't be in that business. I don't want to belabor the point unnecessarily, but for the benefit of some young person who is wondering what to do for a living, please remember that tombstone cutters don't metion how snake charmers find their way into cemeteries. Some snake charmers are reputed to remove not only the fangs but also the bone from which the fangs grow; others sew the snake's mouth shut.

Within the scope of my own memory, at least four American herpetologists have died of a snakebite. It's not a jolly way to go. Herpetologists aside, about a dozen people die each year in the U.S.A. from a snakebite. Alaskans seem to be immune.

Propulsion is a tricky business for a legless, finless, and wingless creature, but the snake has mastered it beautifully. Snakes burrow, race through trees, swim, and even glide short distances through the air with no visible means of flapping or putting one foot in front of the other. Sometimes the motion is so smooth it seems to be done by magic, but high speed motion picture camera studies have demonstrated what happens. No snake can move backward. Remember that a snake has between 100 and 400 vertebrae between its skull and the tip of its tail. Each joint contributes to the flexibility of the whole.

Snakes propel themselves on

Lacking legs, snakes move by use of the numerous ventral scales or scutes. Virtually all snakes have well over 100 ventral scales, with many having 200 or more. Often the number of ventrals is important in identification. Helicops carinicauda. Photo by M. Freiberg.

Chrysopelea ornata, *an Asian snake that actually glides from tree to tree by flattening the body and using it as a parachute. Photo by G. Marcuse.*

land in several ways. If they wish to travel slowly over a rough surface they utilize muscles that connect the ribs to the overlapping belly scales—also known as transverse or abdominal scutes or ventrals. As the muscles move the scales like hinged shingles, the total effect is to push the snake forward. The ribs don't walk. The ribs support the muscles and the muscles drive the hinged belly scales.

For faster locomotion on land, the aforementioned method may be combined with a squirming technique where the snake draws itself into a series of "S" curves and then quickly straightens itself. Because of the arrangement of those belly scales, the path of least resistance is forward.

Some desert snakes need better traction than they can get from sand, so they have developed still another technique to bypass the lack of traction. They lift a coil off the ground and literally throw themselves ahead. In this instance the coil is of necessity on one side or the other and ahead is really aside, so the movement is not toward the snake's head but toward its side. Such a method of moving is called sidewinding, and the snakes are known as sidewinders. Are there left side and right side winders? I don't know.

When snakes swim, most of them do it by one of the first two methods I have described. True sea snakes have developed flattened tails that they are able to sweep from side to side in order to speed their progress through water.

Snakes have nostrils and we do know that their sense of smell is acute, but those nostrils have nothing to do with the sense of smell. The tongue transports odorous substances in the air into the mouth as part of the odor reception process. The nostrils are only for breathing, not smelling.

The tongue of any snake is long, slender, forked, and tapering. It is constantly moving and it serves as an organ of odor reception. There is no relationship between the tongue and venom. The tongue, being moist, is probably sensitive to taste as well

The constantly flicking tongue is the snake's way of picking up information on its environment. Photo by G. Marcuse.

as odor reception. Molecules of odorous substances are caught on the tongue and are carried into the mouth, where the snake does its smelling.

Some snakes have depressions in the area of the nose which we call pits. Vipers with these pits are called pit vipers. These pits are furnished with sensitive nerves that respond to heat so precisely that a warm-blooded animal can be located in the dark by such a snake.

Snakes that glide? Through the air? There are fishes that do it and lizards and squirrels too, so why not a snake? Yes, there is a tree snake that flattens its body to catch some air and it thus parachutes a bit when it wants to move between tree limbs that are spaced beyond its reach.

Snakes that live their entire lives in the sea? Yes, there are a few. All are venomous, some extremely so. Marine snakes are found only in semi-tropical or tropical waters. Their tails are

flattened to aid in swimming, and out of water some species have trouble moving. Most species of sea snakes give birth to living young and so need not even go ashore (like sea turtles) to lay eggs.

Elsewhere you read that snakes accomplish respiration through lungs. All reptiles have lungs, but snakes are unique among animals because many species have but one lung. This situation probably came about to resolve a real estate problem. A snake's shape regulate their body temperature by internal means. This is not quite true. When they hibernate in winter, they are, in a sense, regulating their temperature. Also, when a female python (at least some species) coils herself around her eggs, she does so in order to aid in their incubation. She flexes her muscles, burns a few calories, and her body gets warmer. Please keep an open mind. Bear in mind that even a tuna fish is known to be able to adjust its internal temperature

is so long and narrow that there is hardly room to fit two lungs side by side, and if they were arranged in tandem there would be then the added difficulty of lopsided windpipes, pulmonary arteries, and veins.

When warm-bloodedness versus cold-bloodedness is considered, we call reptiles cold-blooded. We mean to say that reptiles, certainly snakes, cannot

This cleared and stained water snake, Nerodia, *shows the great number of vertebrae and ribs. Photo by Dr. G. Dingerkus.*

somewhat. Of course reptiles, including snakes, can adjust their temperature externally by various behavioral mechanisms, such as basking.

Rattlesnakes—all are found only in the Western Hemisphere,

are all venomous, and all are so named because they accumulate on their tails special rings of dried skin tissue. When a rattler molts its skin, all of it comes off except for a little bit which forms a loose ring on the tail. When the snake vibrates its tail the rings bump each other and generate a sort of hissing, buzzing, or whirring sound. A rattlesnake whose rattles have broken off is still venomous at the other end. Rattles and venom have nothing to do with each other.

Similar noises are generated by snakes without rattles who simply vibrate their tails against dry leaves on the forest floor. Of course many snakes are prone to hiss. Hissing is in no way associated with either venom or with biting. You easily could be bitten by a snake that did not rattle or hiss. Also, you might not be bitten by a snake that did a good deal of hissing and rattling.

The bull snake of the U.S.A. makes another sound, not a rattle or a hiss but (according to some authors) a windy roar that suggests a bovine creature; hence its name. The bull snake makes an interesting pet if adequate room is available.

Did you wonder how the cobra was induced to rise from the basket if it is so hard of hearing and it could not see the snake charmer until its head was above the lip of the basket? My wife, typist and most severe critic (one person in three roles) brought this up. There are three possible answers.

1: The snake lifted its head because the basket lid was removed and the light that poured in woke the animal and stimulated it.

2: Deaf snakes are believed to be able to sense sound as a vibration transmitted through

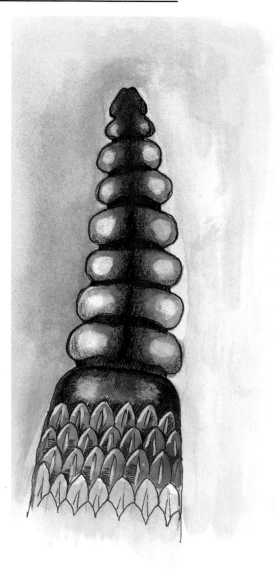

The rattle of a rattlesnake is a group of specialized rings of skin held together by a system of prongs and flanges. The age of a rattlesnake cannot be told with certainty by the number of rattles.

Hibernation

The snake charmer's cobra rises from the basket for several possible reasons. Naja naja.

solids rather than propagated as wave motion through the air.

3: Dr. Richard Zweifel tells me that snakes *can* hear airborne vibrations.

This story has reached a point where I must remind you that natural history is not cut and dried, black or white, all or nothing, absolutely and forever. Nature reflects evolution, and many evolving organisms are around to display and demonstrate the stages that others have passed through. Words like usually, mostly, generally, often, possibly, and probably are the weasel words of naturalists. It is difficult to say never, always, all, absolutely, or every in this business and still be 100% correct.

Hibernation

In winter, snakes from temperate climates will become dormant. They will crawl into hiding places such as caves or they will burrow underground where the temperature remains warmer than freezing until spring. Some species are more tolerant of cold than others, but none can operate effectively if the body temperature goes much below 50° F. Not only is it harder to pump cold blood as it thickens, but digestive fluids are less effective. Also, many of the foods that a snake is accustomed to eat in summer are unavailable in winter. So, in areas where there are cold winters, snakes hibernate and in areas where there is occasional cold weather snakes hibernate less or we might say that they just become lethargic or dormant.

A captive house pet will quickly adjust to its cage temperature; what else can it do? If it is active and has a good appetite, you can assume the temperature range is right for it. If it acts cold, it probably is. You might provide a small electric light on a timer for several hours a day to supplement your home heating for the snake. This will cost but pennies a day and may make the difference between a sick specimen and an active, docile pet. Remember that if you furnish local heating you should also provide an area where the snake can retire from it, in case it gets too hot.

Another technical word you may encounter in literature about reptiles is estivation. This is akin to hibernation, and it is performed by desert animals when the weather is too hot and/or too dry for survival. The creature simply

Old barns and similar piles of lumber and boards provide suitable hiding and estivating sites for many types of snakes. Photo by J. Gee.

buries itself under an insulating layer of earth until the climate is more to its liking.

In localities where snakes must protect themselves against freezing, they will crawl into abandoned burrows of other animals and into caves and basements and foundations of homes. Often a single hibernation site will attract thousands of snakes. Nature lovers go ga-ga over this sort of thing.

So, by way of review, if you keep a snake that is accustomed to hibernate, it will skip the hibernation period and remain

Because snake eggs tend to be adhesive when first laid, they are seldom as clean and white as these, usually being covered with bits of dirt and other debris.

active throughout the year. The length of daylight probably triggers the beginning of hibernation, so you should not only maintain a temperature ranging between 50° and 80° Fahrenheit, but you should hook up a light on a timer to assure no less than ten hours of light out of every 24.

Reproduction

A young snake might come into

the world in one of several ways, depending on how it was with its parent. To begin, a sexually mature female snake is impregnated by a male of the same species. Eggs develop within her body and are then deposited, usually in a cluster, often in a hole or under a log or a rock or some forest floor litter. Sometimes the female stays with her white or creamy eggs to protect (or incubate?) them. This

The easiest snakes to breed in captivity are usually the live-bearing species, such as the garter snakes and boas. This Thamnophis *has just had a large litter.*

is the way with pythons. Most egglaying snakes do not care for the eggs. A snake egg is not hard and brittle like a bird's egg but rather leathery. The eggs, as you might suspect, tend to be long ovals rather than spheres. Most

turtles lay spherical eggs. Snakes that lay eggs are said to be oviparous.

But not all snakes lay eggs. Many, including boas and garters and rattlesnakes and certain sea snakes, give birth to living young. Does this make them viviparous or ovoviviparous? It all depends on the internal hookups before birth. If the embryo received nourishment from the mother, then we would call it viviparous, but if there was no input, then we would say ovoviviparous. In point of fact, some snakes fall into each of these categories.

After the eggs or young are delivered, the female may have another encounter with a male, or she may not. That's right—many female snakes will store male sperm from one mating and produce as many as three litters of living young or clutches of fertile eggs with no additional matings.

Many snakes of the more desirable varieties are listed in dealers' catalogs as "captive born." This does not necessarily mean born of a captive mating. A female snake might produce as many as three or four batches of eggs or litters of young after having mated just once—and that can happen before she was made captive.

Sometimes, and in some places, this designation of captive born is important for legal reasons since certain species are protected by law and may not be captured. The Florida indigo snake is one of many in that category. The legal ramifications are sticky. If in doubt, don't risk confiscation, arrest, and a possible fine.

A livebearing snake gives its young no care or protection. Once born, they are on their own. Egg-layers don't necessarily

Assorted snake eggs in a simple incubator full with vermiculite. Notice the wrinkled shells of the hatched eggs. Photo by J. Gee.

brood or "incubate" their eggs. If you have a female snake who is brooding a clutch of eggs, let her do it. If the eggs were simply buried in wood chips or litter or sand on the cage floor, you might collect them for storage in a smaller container with sufficient vermiculite, leaf mold or sphagnum moss to cover them. The dry absorbent material should be mixed with an equal weight of water. If the eggs are fertile, they will hatch, *with no additional help from you,* in eight to 12 weeks. Birds' eggs are routinely turned but reptile eggs should not be turned.

Remember that if your snake cage is screened the babies might be able to crawl into or through what would stop their mother.

Certainly most albino and many melanistic specimens were captive raised or captive-bred— an albino snake would have a hard time hiding from predators in its natural habitat.

If small snake eggs adhere to the substrate, they can be transferred to the incubator container without trying to free them.

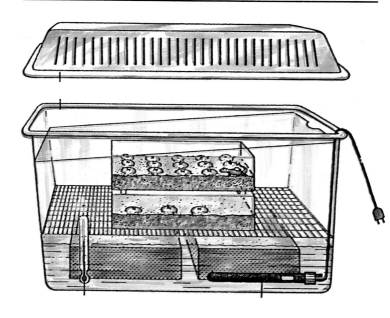

This rather complicated incubator uses water kept at a constant temperature to produce a warm, humid medium suitable for hatching the eggs of many snakes, lizards, and turtles. The eggs are placed on vermiculite in a separate small container.

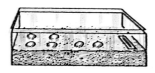

Molting

Surely you have heard of someone who was buying or selling a snake oil remedy. This was back in the "good old days" when we had "cures" for many diseases that now kill people. One of the greatest of these remedies was snake oil. It was generally made available in a small bottle and touted by a gent who was wearing a waxed mustache and a black derby. He was often assisted by an old Indian who was dressed in full chief's regalia.

When a snake has been in his skin for two months or so, his colors will become dull and his eyes will cloud over in a milky blue and he will become morose or mean. Then, overnight, his normal color will return. This may be as a result of that miracle juice—snake oil. It is according to some authorities secreted by the snake underneath the thin layer of outer skin and it serves to lubricate and release the dead epidermis. When the skin is thoroughly molted, it will look especially clean and colorful. This would be the time to photograph it if you want the best colors.

Poisonous and Non-poisonous

All nature is built upon change; much of it is gradual, and many ancient ancestors of common

Every time a snake molts in captivity it is at risk. However, if the humidity of the cage is at the correct level for the species, the snake is generally healthy, and the body is not scarred or deformed, the odds are good that the snake will come through in fine condition.

Poisonous and Non-poisonous

animals are not at all extinct but are still around. We have reason to believe that the first snakes evolved from animals that had legs. This belief is derived in part from a look at the vestigial spurs on a python. We might also reasonably speculate that snake venom is an evolutionary development and further speculate that some ancestors of our most venomous snakes are still around, working with less than the greatest amount of the most toxic substances.

It is a fact that some snake venoms are more toxic than others and some snakes' fangs for injecting these poisons are shorter than those on other snakes. Some poisonous snakes don't have hollow or even grooved fangs for injecting poisonous venom. Some have no fangs at all. These snakes just

Although their venom is exceedingly deadly to humans, kraits are handled with impunity by commercial snake dealers because they virtually never bite. Commonly sold as a food animal in the Orient, most people there consider kraits to be harmless snakes. Bungarus multicinctus. *Photo courtesy R. E. Kuntz.*

chew the poison into the victim. By now I think you are beginning to get the sense of the message. Nature provides us with variety in many shades of gray. Sometimes this variety represents evolutionary change and sometimes it is simply a mutation that never got off the ground, but the end result is often a wide range of values for any particular feature including the amount of damage that a snake can inflict when it bites.

Snakebite, then, may or may not be accompanied by poison. The poison may or may not be toxic enough or in a sufficient dose to kill or damage muscle tissue, blood or nerves. Snakes commonly considered to be harmless may still be able to bite, and the damage caused by such a bite can range from zero to substantial. My father was once bitten on the hand by a water snake and he bled copiously until a compress bandage was applied to the wound. This species of snake is not "venomous," but certainly it could not be called harmless. Its saliva contained an anticlotting agent and so caused the wound to bleed more than a similar break in the skin without the saliva.

There are, in addition to anticoagulants, some snake venom components that cause paralysis of the breathing apparatus, and the victim is thus immobilized and/or killed. Other groups of snakes generate poisons that attack muscle tissue and cause it to disintegrate. Still others produce venom that combines these features. Which is the worst? Does it really matter, once one is dead? Here, to cause or to settle arguments, is a list of some snakes with the quantity and toxicity of their venoms.

Name	Quantity of venom in a snake in milligrams	Milligrams in a lethal dose for a human
Various Sea Snakes	1-15	2-4
Indian Krait	8-20	3
Eastern Coral Snake	3-5	4
Tiger Snake	35-65	3
Australian Brown Snake	5-10	3
Mambas	6-100	12-15
Various Cobras	150-350	18-45
Puff Adder	160-200	95
Gaboon Viper	450-600	180?
American Copperhead	40-70	100
Cottonmouth Moccasin	100-150	125
Rattlesnakes		
Eastern Diamondback	400-700	100
Western Diamondback	200-300	100
Timber	100-150	75
Mojave	50-90	15
Bushmaster	200-400	150

To put this matter of snakebite in perspective, consider these numbers: In one year, worldwide, 300,000 people will be bitten by venomous snakes and 10% or 30,000 will die. Most of the bites and most of the deaths will be in Southeast Asia. There are more venomous snakes there and there are more barefooted people there and there are relatively fewer doctors equipped with antidotes. In the U.S. we can expect 6,700 people to be bitten in any year (probably zero in Maine, Hawaii, and Alaska) and of that number, a dozen will die. I don't want to unnecessarily belabor the point, but one or two of that dozen could be pet keepers or herpetologists who got careless. Not a nice way to die. Remember, however, that there are hundreds of snake species that are not only non-venomous but even less prone to bite than is your pet dog or cat or rabbit or parrot.

When we look into Bambi's eyes we know that it is a kind and gentle animal because its eyes are brown and limpid and the pupils are round. This is not a rule

A boomslang, Dispholidus typus, killing a chameleon. The boomslang is one of the few rear-fangs that has caused human deaths.

The "other" U. S. venomous snake, the eastern coral snake, Micrurus fulvius. *This "candy-cane" snake has caused several fatalities among collectors and children, but usually it does not bite. Photo by K. Lucas, Steinhart Aqu.*

applicable to snakes. There are the mambas, recognized as among the most venomous in all the world, whose eyes have round pupils. On the other hand, the boas and pythons are all non-venomous but their eyes are furnished with narrow vertical slits for their pupils. Rattlesnakes and vipers in general do have vertical pupils, however.

Some snakes generate a venom which attacks nerves, thus causing paralysis of the victim. This type of venom can be purified, refined, and diluted to a state where it has been used to relieve pain. This then is administered to patients who need relief from intense pain but who should not be given opium derivatives, such as morphine, that lead to drug dependency. Certain painful forms of arthritis have been treated in this manner. Also, an affliction of dogs commonly called lick granuloma is treated with a cobra venom extract.

Snakebite antivenin preparation and administration is a pretty complicated subject. It is hard to describe simply and still be correct. Generally, the best treatment will come from prompt injection of an antivenin that was prepared from the same species that did the biting. One problem arises partly because there are so many venomous snake species and partly because often the snake gets away and identification is not absolutely positive. A second problem arises because it would be almost impossible to store antivenin for all the venomous snakes in all the places where a bitten person might be taken. A third problem arises because of the method of creating antivenin. A horse is injected with a very tiny dose of venom. Of course the horse survives; a substance in its bloodstream was generated to negate the effect of the poison. Next, the horse is given a still stronger dose of snake venom and again it survives, in part because it has developed a slight immunity after that first dose. This procedure is kept up until the horse eventually becomes immune to what would have been a lethal dose of venom. Next, some of the blood of the horse is withdrawn in the same manner as when people give blood at a Red Cross bloodmobile. That horse blood contains the antivenin that may help to save a snakebite victim, *BUT* now there is a third problem. This problem arises because some people are allergic to the natural serum in horse blood that also contains the antivenin that may save the victim's life. If a person is sufficiently allergic he might die of horse serum allergy while being cured of the snake venom. *SO* a procedure of testing for horse serum allergy might well be performed before the antivenin is administered *IF* the victim should live so long. I didn't write this with any intention of humor; it certainly

the animals they are accustomed to eating. Bear in mind that wild snakes are accustomed to capturing and subduing the animal life that they must eat. Snakes don't naturally eat animals that have been killed by others. Some species are known as rear-fanged snakes. They have grooved teeth located in the rear of their upper jaws and these teeth are tied to glands that generate venom or other substances that aid in converting another animal into a meal. What

To a toad, a hognose snake is a venomous species. Its venom is very mild and affects only toads and frogs. Heterodon platyrhinos. *Photo by J. K. Langhammer.*

is not a joking matter. Many people have dedicated their lives to maintaining and operating the laboratories where antivenin is produced, and as a result many lives are saved.

Here follows a list of native U.S. snakes that are not considered dangerous to humans but whose saliva is, to some degree, toxic to

other substances? Well, for instance, a lubricating saliva helps any snake when a mouse or bird or a lizard gets started on its final trip. For another example, consider a saliva (read this as mild venom) that prevents the clotting of blood.

Black-striped snake, *Coniophanes imperialis* — Its bite has been reported to cause itching, numbness, burning sensations, and swelling.

Eastern hognose snake, *Heterodon platyrhinos* — Produces a mild venom that immobilizes frogs and toads. This

species rarely bites people and is generally considered to be a safe pet.

Night snake, *Hypsiglena torquata,* and cat-eyed snake, *Leptodeira septentrionalis* — Both produce a mildly toxic saliva to subdue frogs and lizards.

Northern water snake, *Nerodia sipedon* (and perhaps all of this genus) — Secretes a saliva that acts as an anti-coagulant and thus induces bleeding of wounds caused by its bite.

Mexican vine snake, *Oxybelis aeneus* — Has grooved rear fangs that inject an immobilizing poison into small animals.

Pine woods snake, *Rhadinaea flavilata* — Is reported to produce a saliva that is mildly toxic to small animals.

Mexican black-headed snake, *Tantilla atriceps* — Has two rear fangs that are grooved, and its saliva is mildly toxic, though it is believed to be totally harmless to humans. This may be true of all snakes in the genus *Tantilla.*

Lyre snake, *Trimorphodon*

Tantilla nigriceps *is a small southwestern U. S. black-headed snake that is rear-fanged and theoretically venomous. Photo by R. L. Holland.*

All rattlesnakes, regardless of size, are definitely dangerous. Even the smallest species could kill a child.

biscutatus—Also produces a mild venom to subdue its prey. It is delivered from grooved rear teeth.

At present, there is no evidence that any American boa, whipsnake, kingsnake, milk snake, bull snake, corn snake, ringneck, indigo, or blacksnake, racer, gopher snake, or scarlet snake produces any poison or dangerous saliva that is a threat to humans. A few very mild envenomations have been produced by garter snakes, but they might be due to individual allergies.

In North America *all* rattlesnakes, coral snakes, cottonmouths, and copperheads are recognized as venomous throughout their *entire* lives, even at birth and even after they have been run over by automobiles.

Someone, somewhere will be chewed upon by a so-called non-venomous snake and will suffer a reaction ranging from mild irritation to death. No one has any good reason for letting any snake chew on any person.

Cages

An aquarium is often used to house a small snake. It is easy to clean, relatively inexpensive, and needs only a screen cover and a fastening device to do its job. Unfortunately, it was designed to hold water and not to permit the easy *circulation* of air. Ideally a cage for snakes should have not one but two screened exposures.

Granted, most pet snakes are kept successfully in aquariums, but as your skills and knowledge improve you should not lose sight of this inherent shortcoming of a container with five out of its six sides completely sealed.

The part of the cage you open to gain access to your pet is where it will try to escape. Why?

Very plain tanks are probably best for keeping most snakes. The substrate can be simply put in and a water bowl provided, or the tank can be partitioned into dry and wet sections by a simple divider.

Well, for one thing, snakes don't play games, don't gnaw on toys, don't create nests or sand castles. They rest a lot, eat a little, and constantly, restlessly, and relentlessly explore, poke, and probe. If there is a slight opening or weakness or looseness in the cage, your snake will find and exploit it — even to the extent of rubbing all the skin off its nose.

I suggest that your snake cage be provided with a cover that is secured with a key lock or a combination lock. These animals are often a magnet for stupid or misinformed people who will remove, release, or harass a snake. There are all sorts of horror stories about snakes that were abused by fools and about people who were abused by fools with snakes — don't risk a problem.

If you house your snake in an all-glass aquarium, the screen cover can be hinged and provided with a lock by the use of silicone rubber cement. Your friendly local glazier or hardware supplier can help you accomplish this task.

With a little effort the plain cage can be made more attractive yet still functional. The bromeliads should be planted in such a way that they can be replaced frequently.

The hinge and the hasp can both be cemented in place with a silicone cement and in a few days it will have cured into a permanent connection.

A cage should not be painted with any aromatic coating or preservative. If after the paint has dried there is any residual odor, watch out — it will probably be toxic and perhaps even lethal to your snake. High on the list, but not alone, are the phenolic compounds such as carbolic acid and creosote.

There are accounts in the newspapers from time to time about firemen and plumbers who find boa constrictors or anacondas in bathtubs. This is not a book for people who elect to keep a snake in a bathtub, but it might be appropriate here to mention that some snakes do like to bathe and some snakes, when about to molt, will soak themselves in water, perhaps to help the old outer layer of skin to peel off. Incidentally, under ideal conditions the entire skin covering, from nostrils to tip of tail, will come off in one piece, inside-out.

Terrariums

This is a difficult and controversial subject if you are already an experienced snake keeper. If you are a beginner, just *take my advice.* Keep it *simple.* Keep it *dry.* Keep it *clean.* Keep it *uncrowded.*

Simple: Avoid tricky enclosures

strong and very agile — a heavy stone standing on edge will surely be knocked over and your pet will be injured or the cage will be breached and an escape will result. Snakes are not easily confined.

Dry: Even the giant South American water snake, the anaconda, can be maintained in a dry cage. For still other reasons, the native U.S. water snakes (*Nerodia*) are not recommended for beginners. Many snake diseases like fungus are associated with wet, damp, or moist cages. Dry cages are less likely to be smelly cages. There are plenty of great dry habitats

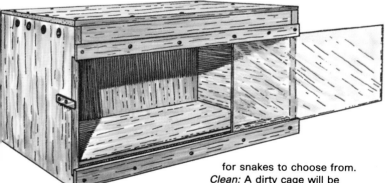

An old-style homemade snake cage with a sliding glass door. Although not particularly attractive, such cages are still considered by many to be the best.

for snakes to choose from.

Clean: A dirty cage will be smelly and it will attract flies, roaches, and other unpleasant insects.

Uncrowded: Many snakes are cannibals and many others that make good pets also don't make good cagemates. A kingsnake will strike terror into the heart of any other species. If you have but one snake, it will certainly not contract the disease of another. Also, remember that many snakes will grow in captivity and that a little bull snake in a five-gallon aquarium will soon grow to be a big fellow who would like to be in a cage nearly as large as a bath tub.

and tricky accessories. Provide a perch or hiding place, absorbent material on the floor, a sturdy container for drinking water, and a removable bath tub. You should be able to sterilize the hardware and throw away the rest in order to reduce unpleasant odors and eliminate mites and ticks. Remember that snakes are quite

Diseases

Ticks are often found on snakes either collected in the wild or recently imported. Some are similar to the common dog ticks, but others are very small and look like large mites under the edges of the scales.

Diseases

Don't assume for even a moment that because snakes are cold-blooded, dry, scaly, and practically mute that they are also disease-free. This is not so. There is but one small ray of sunshine — the diseases of snakes don't seem to be the same as those of people. It is surely improbable and maybe even impossible for a snake to catch a disease from you or *vice versa.*

Now for the bad news. Chilled snakes are prone to pneumonia. Warm such an animal to 80° F. and isolate it from all other reptiles. Your veterinarian might prescribe and administer an antibiotic, and maybe it will help.

Mites and ticks infest and bother wild snakes, and on captive specimens these same parasites can cause the same snakes to die. Ticks can be removed with tweezers, but if you do it that way, often the head of the tick remains embedded deeply in the skin and causes secondary infection. Try to kill the tick by coating it with petroleum jelly or a heavy vegetable oil — this should cause the tick to suffocate and come loose in one piece. It takes a few days to smother a tick; be patient.

Mites can be eliminated with a preparation known as Dri-Die, but you must first be certain that the manufacturer has not added any insecticide in the formula. Substances such as malathion, rotenone, and DDT are not to be used on snakes or in their cages. Some snake keepers report good results by hanging a "No-Pest" strip in the cage for a few days.

There is no sense in killing the ticks and mites on the snake unless its cage or aquarium is also freed of them and their eggs. Live steam is effective but hard to control. Ammonia and hot water will do a good job if you are thorough and apply plenty of elbow grease. Remember not to put the old branches and rocks back into the cage — they surely will be infested also.

Mouth rot is usually a fungus infection that attacks areas that were injured. For example, a snake that rubbed its snout raw on a cage cover is fair game for an attack of mouth rot. Again, antibiotics, especially sulfamethiazine, are effective. This latter drug might be available as a liquid 2 1/2% solution in water. You might irrigate the snake's mouth daily with a wash or spray until the condition is cleared up.

Some snakes in damp cages will develop blisters. Clean and dry the cage and keep it dry and clean. Drain the blisters and wipe the affected area with 50% ethyl alcohol. A good substitute, more readily available, is vodka just as it comes out of the bottle. Wipe it

Contrast in cages. Above is a fancy "state of the art" self-contained cage often used for expensive boas and venomous species. At the right is a simple but very effective molded fiberglass cage of a very popular type.

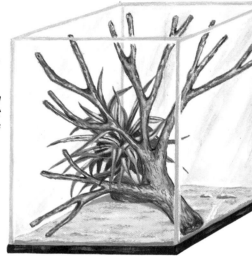

Even terrestrial snakes enjoy curling up on a low branch or piece of wood to bask. Arboreal species of course must have climbing branches to make them feel at home.

on twice daily with a wad of absorbent cotton. Mercurochrome is also an effective antiseptic for minor skin lesions.

If a snake accumulates several layers of unshed skin, you should take it that this animal is poorly nourished or that something else is radically wrong. Confine the snake in a damp burlap bag for three or four days. This might help start the molting process.

Vinegar in the bath water tends to reduce the chance of skin problems. A quick dip in a 50% vinegar-water bath is recommended by some experienced snake keepers. Others suggest a dip in a 3 or 4%

seawater salt solution to control skin lesion problems. I don't know which is best, but I suspect the vinegar would be most effective against fungus infections. A dry cage, bone dry, will also help control this disease.

There are whole books available on this subject. Most are morbid, and many are technical and difficult to read. You would be well advised to start with *one* healthy snake in a clean dry cage. Then, with good temperature control, wholesome food, and humane treatment, your pet easily could live 20 years with no need for medicines.

Most disease among captive snakes is associated with damp

Molded plastic hide boxes are now commercially available.

and dirty cages. You might rightly ask why a snake that was taken from a swamp or a bog doesn't do well in a mini-mimic of this environment. The answer is a compound one. First, a moist terrarium, aquarium, cage or whatever you call it is a poor approximation of the Great Outdoors. The air in an enclosure doesn't circulate as much. Fungus spores and bacteria are recirculated rather than dispersed. An enclosure is frequently glazed, and as a result a good deal or most or all the beneficial antiseptic effects of ultraviolet light in sunlight are lost. The animal is forced to

Ceramic logs and other ornaments are easier to keep clean than the real things and help prevent mite infestations.

remain in close proximity with its excrement and all the bacteria and fungus that dwell on it. Most animal wastes are magnets for decomposition processes as long as the moisture content is over 7%. As organic material becomes less moist, its decay processes slow down. Look at the mummies in Egyptian tombs; some have remained pristine for three or four thousand years.

Face it — a mini-mimic of the habitat that you believe the snake had been thriving in is not necessarily the best way to house your pet. Some experienced and successful fanciers provide absolutely artificial accommodations consisting of disposable paper and easily disinfected metal, glass and painted wood.

As you get started you should set your mind on hygiene and prevention rather than on medical cures for preventable diseases.

Albinos

Indian fakirs will paint eyes and mouth on the tail of a blunt-ended

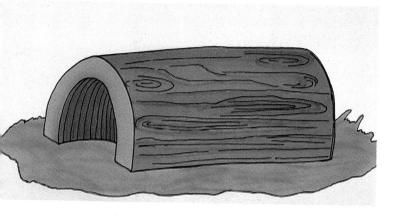

boa and tell the unsuspecting that they are looking at a two-headed snake. Now, that's a fake. A pale or white snake is an albino. It is not a fake. It is an unusual mutant that shows up from time to time in all the higher animals. There are albino mice, rabbits, birds, fishes, and even elephants. In a wild environment these animals have a hard time of it. They often have poor vision and sunburn vulnerability. Some have poor stamina as well. In captivity, however, they often do quite nicely. Captive albino snakes have always attracted a lot of attention and usually command a premium price.

A true albino has pink eyes and no pigment in its skin. Sometimes Mother Nature delivers up a faded or diluted color creature that is almost but not quite an albino. Sometimes still another mutation of genetic material results in an animal that is darker or blacker than normal; call this condition "melanism." If you need an example, perhaps you have seen a gray squirrel that was quite black; this is a good example of melanism. About 40 years ago I seem to remember that there were a bunch of these squirrels on the campus of the University of Illinois at Urbana.

Temperature
A snake generates little or no internal heat and it doesn't perspire, so it must rely on its environment to furnish the desired range of temperatures. When you confine a snake you

An albino Thamnophis sirtalis *can be a gorgeous sight. Many albino snakes are now bred in captivity and are readily available for a price. Photo by K. Lucas, Steinhart Aqu.*

44

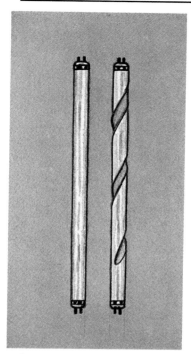

If snakes are to reproduce in captivity, proper lighting is essential. Plant lights will not work.

Desert terraria are perhaps the hardest to properly maintain as they require a careful control of lighting and humidity. Additionally, desert snakes tend to hide during the day.

must provide what it would seek out for itself if it were on its home turf.

Since your best guess, best heat source, and best heat control are probably less than perfect from the standpoint of a snake, you should arrange the cage for your captive so that it can find the area that offers the right temperature.

An electric light on a timer to provide perhaps ten hours of light and warmth might be a good starting point. How many watts? Well, that depends on the average temperature of the room. If you have a temperate zone snake in the living area of your home, the necessary wintertime additional heat might be obtained from a 15 or 20 watt lamp.

A tropical snake in a cooler room might need 50 or more watts to keep it comfortable. If the daytime temperature is too low, the snake will be lethargic and disinterested in food. It may have trouble digesting what it has eaten. An error of ten degrees on your part could cause the premature death of your pet.

This is not to say that a snake cannot tolerate a range of more than 10° Fahrenheit (5 ½° Centigrade or Celsius). What you need to determine is the comfort range of your animal and then avoid going more than 10°F. over or under that range. A garter snake, for example, would do nicely if the temperature varied daily between 50 and 70° F. It would still survive if the temperature dropped to 40 or went up to 80 once in a while. A tropical boa might call for a 65 to 85° F. range. If you use a thermometer and carefully employ your powers of observation you can quickly determine what your pet prefers. Place the warming light at one end of the cage and then see where the snake settles down. Remember that you can hook up a light on a timer to provide daytime light and warmth and you can additionally control this same light with a high-temperature thermostatic cut-off. A pet shop should be able to get you such a thermostat. Remember that you do not want a thermostatically controlled aquarium heater. All you want is the thermostat.

There are many ingenious heating pad devices on the market (some are offered for brooding chicks or for dog kennels or for nursing pigs). I suggest you start with a small inexpensive incandescent light in a warm room until you know better what your animal needs.

Small specimens of tropical pythons and boas, such as this hatchling Python reticulatus, *are more sensitive to changes of temperature than larger specimens and more likely to be adversely affected by sudden temperature drops. Photo by P. J. Stafford.*

Feeding

No snake will eat grain or vegetables or fruit or mushrooms. There is a famous old story about a horse who was gradually trained to eat sawdust, but unfortunately about that time he dropped dead. Feed your snake on animal food. Preferably feed it on *whole* animals as contrasted to strips of beef muscle or fillets of boneless fish.

A snake's digestive system is designed to handle shells, scales, bones, hair, and feathers. Some species even eat whole birds' eggs; later they may regurgitate the shells. The advantage of providing your pet with such whole organisms as whole fish, whole rodents, whole insects, or whatever is that the trace vitamins and elements that accumulate in certain bones and organs will also be available for assimilation. A wild snake doesn't pluck feathers or skin mice or fillet fish. It eats the whole thing.

A *whole* mouse for a kingsnake or a rat snake or a corn snake *is* a "balanced" diet. A *whole* shiner or killie or smelt or eel or mummichog *is* a "balanced" diet for a water snake or a garter snake. A *whole* toad *is* a "balanced" diet for a hognose snake. Do I make my point?

Is it necessary to feed live animals to your pet snake? Absolutely not. They need not even be freshly killed. You might accumulate mice (in plastic zip-locked bags) in the freezer and then thaw a meal to room temperature when you wish to feed your snake.

Don't buy expensive goldfish to feed to snakes. Your pet will do at least as well on bait-fish at much less cost. Again, the fish can be fresh-frozen and then thawed thoroughly before they are fed.

If you purchase a snake from a

Species that feed almost exclusively on a single type of food are usually hard to keep. Unless you have toads available all year around, it will be very hard to keep a hognose over the winter. Heterodon platyrhinos. *Photo by J. Dodd.*

pet dealer, make him *show* you the feeding process. No talk, just show. Some captive snakes refuse to feed themselves and must be force-fed to maintain life. Some snakes will regurgitate what they were force-fed. This is not a situation you should start out with. Your first snake should be a self-feeder if you buy it from another snake keeper or from a pet dealer.

Assume the worst, that you caught or were given a non-venomous snake that you have caged. It hasn't eaten and now you believe it is hungry and needs to be fed. What to do? First identify the species positively. This is important since some species have special natural diets. For example, a hognose will eat a toad avidly. Most other snakes cannot tolerate toads because of a noxious liquid in the skin of a toad. The second step is to assure that you can obtain this required food throughout the year at a price you can afford to pay.

If your snake naturally eats rodents, it remains for you to provide the appropriate *size* rodent. A snake that eats small rats will also eat hamsters, gerbils, and mice. A snake that eats large rats will also eat small rabbits (although, technically, a rabbit is not a rodent) or guinea pigs.

Pay strict attention to the source of your supply of rodents. If they were killed by poison, you certainly should not feed them to your snake.

If a snake encounters a rat, the scenario could go about like this: First the rat might have been killed by constriction or by injection of venom. Still other species of snakes will eat living prey. A captive snake could be offered an already dead rat at room temperature or slightly

warmer. The rat might be an inch and a half in diameter and the neck of the snake might be but five-eighths or three-quarters of an inch in diameter. Don't worry. The rat will fit. Even if the snake were a bit thinner, it would still fit.

The snake will probably take the rat by its nose and fasten its upper and lower teeth on one side. Then it will advance its jaws on the other side and take another purchase. There will be no bone crushing involved. The operation is a slow, methodical creeping motion, alternating from side to side. Some saliva might appear as the snake lubricates the rat to ease its passage. The lower jaws will soon be so displaced that most of the work will seem to come from the upper jaws and the throat. The snake's

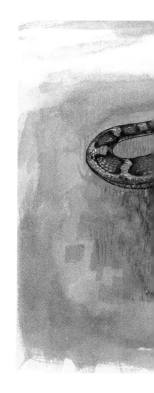

eyes will bulge and its neck will stretch until the scales are widely separated.

The snake will stop to rest from time to time. Eventually the entire rat will be inside the snake. Then the snake might yawn a few times. Depending on how large the snake was in proportion to the size of its meal, it might want to eat again in a few days or it might not be really hungry for perhaps several weeks. Raymond L. Ditmars tells us that a 20-foot python (which would have weighed a little more than 200 pounds) swallowed a 40-pound pig with some difficulty. That same snake, according to Ditmars, would usually eat two or three chickens at a meal, with such meals at intervals of 60 days. For another example from Ditmars, a regal python 16 feet long would eat an eight-pound rooster — head, feather, spurs, the whole thing — in ten minutes and immediately be ready to eat some more. A considerable number of species of snakes feed at least in part on reptiles and amphibians.

Glossy snakes eat lizards.

Garter snakes eat frogs and salamanders.

Milk snakes eat worm snakes and many other species as well, including venomous snakes. A

The most keepable snakes are those that will feed regularly on living or frozen small rodents and chicks. This is one of the reasons the various species of Elaphe *and* Lampropeltis *are so popular.*

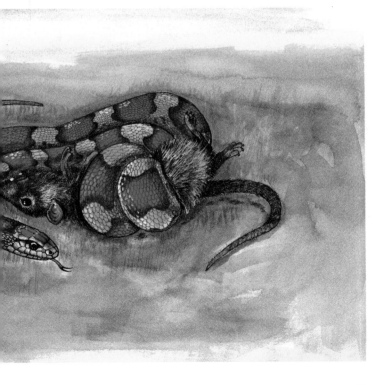

milk snake is a variety of kingsnake, so we should not be surprised.

Scarlet snakes eat the eggs of snakes and other reptiles.

Racers eat frogs, lizards, and other snakes.

The black-striped snake eats toads, frogs, lizards, and snakes.

Ringnecks eat salamanders, lizards, and small snakes.

The indigo snake eats small

Young rainbow snakes eat tadpoles and salamanders.

Hognose snakes eat toads, lizards, snakes and reptile eggs.

Night snakes eat lizards and frogs.

Kingsnakes eat snakes, lizards and frogs. The common kingsnake will eat copperheads, coral snakes, and rattlers! Kingsnakes will also eat mice, birds, and eggs. The kingsnakes

turtles, frogs, and snakes, even venomous snakes. It seems to be immune to snake venom. It is not itself venomous. Note that wild native indigo snakes are among the protected species and you will not be permitted to possess them.

Rat snakes eat lizards.

Mud snakes eat eels almost exclusively. Eels are fishes, not reptiles, but sometimes people get confused.

Next to rodents and chicks, lizards are probably the most standard snake food. Common species of Sceloporus are readily available or captured in many parts of the country. Photo by Dr. G. Dingerkus.

are probably our most avid native snake eaters.

The cat-eyed snake eats frogs and lizards.

Whipsnakes eat lizards and snakes.

Water snakes eat frogs, tadpoles, and snakes in addition to their main entree item — fishes.

The saddled leafnose snake feeds mostly on lizards.

The spotted leafnose snake preferentially dines on banded geckos and the eggs of these geckos.

The pine woods snake eats frogs and lizards almost exclusively.

The long-nosed snake of Texas and other western states eats lizards, small snakes, and reptile eggs.

The swamp snake eats sirens, tadpoles, and frogs.

The lyre snake eats lizards.

Most venomous snakes eat mammals, birds and fishes, but the cottonmouth will also eat sirens and frogs and other snakes. Since this is not a book for keepers of dangerous snakes, I will not go into their diet. Suffice it to say that this list makes it clear that many North American snakes feed on others of their ilk. The shape of a snake makes a convenient fit for the shape of the stomach of another snake.

After all that listing of snakes that eat amphibians and reptiles, maybe I should say that snakes don't always know their limitations, or maybe they do know and it is only we who do not know. There have been occasions

when a small snake was attacked simultaneously by two larger snakes and when the chomping was all over, only one very swollen large snake remained in the cage.

Should you feed your pet snake on live birds and mammals? I don't recommend it and I believe that most people who are experienced with these animals would agree. If the food is freshly killed or promptly frozen after it was killed and then thoroughly thawed, it should be perfectly adequate as food for your snake. Worms are usually served alive to small snakes, but one good reason not to feed a live mouse or rat to a snake is that if the snake is not ready to eat, the rodent might bite or even kill the snake. Remember that your cage is not quite the Great Outdoors. You have created an artificial environment and that's the way it is.

When we have to feed small snakes, our thoughts automaticlly

go to earthworms and more earthworms and then for many people, our thoughts sort of fizzle. Well, that's O.K. for garter snakes, but when it comes to the gentle and lovely little green snake a worm isn't its thing. The books say "insects." The problem that arises is that when we send a kid into a field to bring us some insects to feed our snake, that kid will nearly always bring back crickets and grasshoppers. A green snake will probably eat a cricket now and again, especially if it gets one that just molted, but a steady diet of hard-shelled bugs is not ideal for such a snake. The green snake would probably do well with soft hairless caterpillars in its diet. What about winter in northern climes? Well, you might try recently molted silkworms, mealworms, and crickets. These you can buy through reptile suppliers, some pet dealers or from dealers in fish baits. I don't recommend a ringneck or a green snake as a pet for a beginner.

There is an African snake which is accustomed to eating bird eggs. It does so without wasting a drop, even if the egg was just freshly laid. The technique is ingenious. The egg is swallowed whole. It is not broken by the snake's teeth. In fact, the snake that specializes in this sort of thing has very few teeth! The shell is not broken until the egg has reached the esophagus of the snake, well on its way to the stomach. Several sections of backbone (vertebra) are furnished with sharp hard points that

Crickets are readily available but they are not eaten by that many species of snakes. They can be used to feed food lizards, however.

extend into the digestive tract. When the egg gets to them, the snake flexes its muscles and the shell is penetrated and broken by those sharp points. This snake then often but not necessarily regurgitates just the dry shell. This snake is *Dasypeltis*, consisting of five species. It is found in Africa and southwestern Arabia. A snake but 30 inches long is easily able to get itself around a chicken's egg.

North American snakes that eat reptiles and it showed a large snake and a crew of husky men who were straightening out its kinks. Also shown was a greased pole with a bunch of rabbits stretched out along its length. The snake was about to have a meal placed in its stomach. Some zoo specimens are so valuable that they cannot be permitted to starve themselves, and yet, if left alone, they might do just that. Such a meal might be administered only three times a

Force-feeding of snakes is usually considered a last resort. Various complicated pieces of equipment are available to make the often messy job easier.

eggs don't have this special equipment, so they usually limit themselves to relatively smaller eggs.

Fifty years ago I was intrigued by a photograph of a python about to be fed. This picture appeared in a popular book about

year and such a snake might or might not eventually eat willingly without any further encouragement.

You might have to resort to some force-feeding with your newly obtained snake, but for most of the species that a beginner should start with, the snake will avidly feed itself as soon as it becomes tame and accustomed to its surroundings.

If you have a small hognose or milk snake or garter that hasn't eaten in a week or two, you might try to get it started with a broomstraw and an earthworm. With the straw you should gently but firmly open the snake's mouth and while it is open lay the worm across the jaws. Then close the mouth over the worm and the straw and slide the straw out, leaving the worm inside the snake's closed mouth. Hold the jaws closed for a half minute, gently lower the snake to the floor of its cage, and quietly and slowly

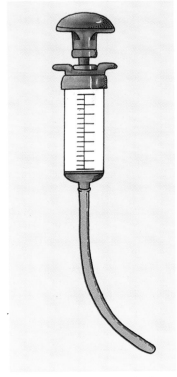

One of the simplest force-feeders is a syringe with a long plastic tube on the end. Snakes should not be force-fed unless they cannot be returned to the wild before winter.

release your grip on its jaws. It is highly likely that your snake will quickly eat that earthworm and it is also highly likely that the snake

will take the next worm you offer without any help from the broomstraw. Frogs and mice can be started down the mouths of larger snakes with a tongue depressor or the stick from an ice cream bar.

If you have a snake that refuses to eat voluntarily you can resort to force-feeding, but if it is a local native you should release the animal.

Ideally, the aim of every animal keeper is to avoid force-feeding. Perhaps the snake doesn't eat because it is nocturnal and you offer the food in broad daylight. Perhaps the temperature is too low or too high. Perhaps you are offering the wrong food. Perhaps the food is stale. Perhaps the snake is uncomfortable in its cage because it is crowded or damp or nervous for lack of a place to hide. Perhaps you have too many snakes and not enough time to watch the animal, its appearance, and its behavior. Is there another larger snake in the same cage or in a nearby cage that frightens your pet? Simple problems, simple answers; most can be answered by applying some simple God-given intelligence.

When you move a snake to new quarters, put it in a soft cloth bag like a sturdy pillowcase. Place the whole package in the cage, untied, and leave it strictly alone for as long as it takes for the snake to come out of its own free will. This might take an hour or it might take as long as a week. Don't push. The snake might hide in the folds of the bag and only come out occasionally from time to time, or it might spend a good deal of its time in the open and only crawl into or under the cloth occasionally and for short periods. Let a snake new to its surroundings take its time getting acclimated. Remember, no cage

Many tropical species will feed readily on frozen and thawed mice. Oxybelis fulgidus. *Photo by M. Freiberg.*

is quite like the Great Outdoors.

Something of a revolution in snake keeping has taken place in these last 20 or 30 years. At one time a snake that was known to eat mice would be offered only live mice. Snakes known to eat frogs were offered only live frogs,

etcetera. Now we know better. For most snakes, a fresh-killed or a freshly thawed mouse or frog is just as nutritious and just as avidly eaten as a live specimen. The mice might be killed by sealing in a small jar with a screw cap; the frogs might be killed by placing them in a plastic zip-lock bag and then freezing the package, or they might be dispatched by a process known as pithing (a needle is driven into

the vertebral column, where it severs all connections to and communication with the brain; any high school biology teacher can teach you how to do it).

Be aware that a snake that relishes a green frog or a bullfrog or a leopard frog may not be able to eat an American toad or a Fowler's toad, or worse yet, a pickerel frog, *Rana palustris*. This latter species of frog produces a toxic secretion through its skin so toxic that other animals in the same aquarium will soon sicken and die. Know the pickerel frog and steer clear of it.

Natives versus Exotics

You caught a garter snake or a milk snake or whatever and you are keeping it as a caged pet. Great! Now you begin to look for something bigger or prettier or just something different. Should you aim at an imported snake from some exotic place or should you limit your hobby to native snakes? This is *not* a good question. The national origin of a snake is far less important than several other factors. Please

Be careful when feeding or even handling certain frogs and toads. Some amphibians, such as Bufo marinus, *shown here, have very potent skin secretions. Photo by H. Schultz.*

consider them before you make a selection:

1: You should not keep a venomous snake as a pet.

2: You should obey the laws regarding protected, rare, and endangered species. Many snakes don't reproduce in captivity and are already so scarce that they must be left alone if they are to survive.

3: You should choose a variety that is recognized as hardy and easy to feed.

4: You should choose a species that is of a convenient size and will not grow to an inconvenient size. There are beautiful constrictors that grow to as much as a reported 30 feet. Well, even 15 feet and a couple of hundred pounds is quite a snake. There are other equally beautiful species that will coil up nicely in the palm of your hand.

5: You should choose a species for which proper food is readily available. Ideally a snake should be fed what it is accustomed to eat if it were not a captive. Fish, worms, frogs, crawfish, and mice are easy to come by, but other snakes, lizards, small eels, and small birds may be overly expensive or hard for you to get. Actually, newly hatched chicks can be purchased from a hatchery and kept frozen until needed for a meal — bird eaters will do well on thawed chicks if the size is right.

6: You should choose a snake you can afford to lose. Snake life is measured in years, between three and at most 25 or 30. You may be buying an animal in its later years. If it expires, could you buy another without hocking the family jewels?

In summary, you should choose a snake whose color, shape, cost, size, disposition, and food requirements are what you want for a pet and you need not concern yourself with its national origin.

Prices of Snakes

Don't own what you cannot afford to lose. Very few captive snakes live much longer than 20 years, and that figure is probably higher than it would be for a snake in the native habitat. Nevertheless, all life is in continual hazard, and snakes do die.

A 1985 price list from a recognized dealer tells us that an albino Burmese python 9 feet long was available for $20,000 — that is *twenty thousand dollars!* Other snakes are of course much less expensive . . . but there are none that are really *cheap.* I should mention at this point that the U.S. Fish and Wildlife Service monitors this business and tolerates no

commercial trading in rare or endangered species.

Few dealers want to bother with varieties of snakes that retail for less than $20 because then they end up competing with kids in the neighborhood who are out catching them after school.

A price list that includes an albino Burmese python for $20,000 might give you some great ideas, especially if your present place of employment is a tooth paste factory or a used car lot. Well, don't quit your present job, however unrewarding, in order to become a proprietor of an albino Burmese python snake

Delicate foreign species are seldom a good buy unless you are really an advanced hobbyist. Just because a snake is offered for sale does not mean it can be successfully kept. Coronella austriaca. *Photo courtesy Dr. D. Terver, Nancy Aqu.*

farm. I've known quite a few people in these businesses of snake farm — herpetological supply — private zoo — Frank Buck Bring 'Em Back Alive. They were knowledgeable, industrious, dedicated, and relatively poor. Certainly none I knew were driving Mercedes Benz touring cars or vacationing on the Riviera.

Prices of Snakes

Commercial raising of snakes is feasible today but requires much room and devotion. Albino corn snakes and California kingsnakes are commonly raised for sale, as are tricolored kingsnakes and milk snakes. Photo by R. W. Applegate.

Granted, a $20,000 python is something to contemplate but: 1: There are not many around, nor are there likely to be. And 2: there are not many customers around either, nor are there likely to be.

A goodly number of rare and unusual reptiles are kept and sometimes bred in zoos throughout the world. These animals replenish stocks lost to age or disease in other institutions. This is accomplished by trades between curators or directors of these institutions, so many exhibition quality animals never enter the market place. Most of the dealers, and there aren't many in all the world, cater to these zoos and also to a relatively small group of well-to-do private reptile fanciers. This is much like the diamond business or the rare coin business. One doesn't simply hang up a shingle and watch the world beat a pathway to his door. If you want such a business, I suggest you would do better by building mousetraps.

The capture of wild reptiles for this trade is usually carried out in wild and exotic places by semi-professionals who have to be there for some other reason — tea farmers, pineapple farmers, rubber tree farmers, rural bus operators, shop keepers, and so on. They find a snake or someone offers them one that had been caught locally. It is passed from hand to hand with transportation costs and a little profit added at each exchange until it gets to a licensed and bonded wholesale exporter of wild animals in Singapore, Hong Kong, Bombay, Nairobi, or Manaus. From there it will go by air to Hamburg, London, Miami, or New York and through another wholesaler to a dealer or a zoo.

Imagine what it must have been like to move exotic animals in sailing ship days when it took several weeks just to cross the North Atlantic. Now a python from Burma can be air-delivered to Chicago within four days!

Right: Uncommon or rarely imported foreign species can be found on occasion in many pet shops. Lycodon striatus bicolor. Photo by B. Kahl.

Incidentally, at present there are no extended quarantine periods for snakes entering the U.S.A. A bird might have to wait in isolation for a month, but a snake can come right in. This is ironic since a bird would need daily feeding whereas a snake could go a month without a meal and be none the worse for the experience. As a matter of fact, there are many captive snakes that are fed regularly only once a month or even less frequently.

Snakes in Commerce

Do you wonder about canned snake meat? Yes, rattler is considered good, but I never heard about anyone becoming wealthy in that business.

Do you wonder about breeding snakes for the pet trade? Yes, there is some commerce in captive-bred snakes, but there are so many hobbyists who have a surplus of cage-bred specimens that a snake farm could operate only as a money-losing hobby.

Do you want to deal in venoms to be used in medicine? Here the market is saturated by government supported programs in many nations. You put your life on the line every time you milk a snake for venom. Are you really cut out for this sort of thing?

Do you want to deal in snakeskins for the leather trade? There are many shoes, wallets, and handbags made from snakeskin, but most of this material comes from South America, India, and Southeast Asia where really big snakes come cheap.

Do you want to deal in snake eyes? Here, finally, is a business for anyone. There is less risk gambling with dice than investing in snake breeding schemes.

Snakes are indeed kept and even bred just to be milked for their venom, which is used in producing antivenins and various drugs, but this is certainly not an occupation for a hobbyist. A bite from this puff adder, Bitis, *would probably result in death in a few hours.*

The Scientific Side

Scientific Words

Let's begin with "herpetology." This word is derived from the Greek. Herpes is the word for crawling things, and we apply it to reptiles and amphibians. Ology means study, so herpetology is the study of reptiles and amphibians. In the same manner, ornithology is the scientific study of birds and ichthyology of fishes.

One big step in science is to give names to living things. This he accomplished in 1758, and since then it has been accepted throughout the scientific world. We are fortunate that his system works so well because by now so many thousands upon thousands of living forms have been described and classified that any new system would call for rewriting a tremendous mass of scientific literature.

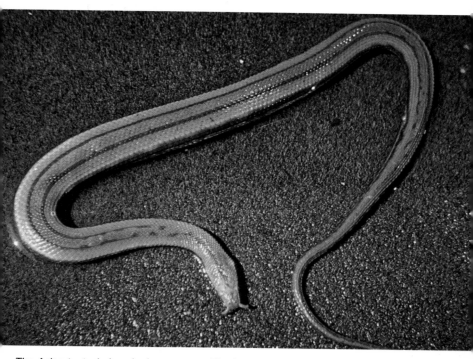

The Asian tentacled snake bears the unusual generic name Erpeton, *which is based on the French spelling of "herpeton." Thus the name of this snake literally means "crawling animal." Photo by J. K. Langhammer.*

give names to living things. We credit a Swedish botanist, Carl Linné (Linnaeus) (1707-1778), with the final design of the system for naming and classifying all living

The beauty of what Linné did is to be found both in its firmness and in its flexibility. It offers us a consistent way to name every organism. It gives us an outline that Charles Darwin, almost a hundred years later, could use as he laid out his theory of evolution. It also permits, in its present form, changes of name to suit new knowledge. Were it not so flexible, it would have failed.

Linné's native tongue was hardly

Scientific names of snakes sometimes change. Until the 1940's, the common garter snake, Thamnophis sirtalis, *was widely called* Thamnophis ordinatus. *Photo by K. Lucas, Steinhart Aqu.*

known outside of Sweden, and since all European science was already being conducted in Latin, he used that language in his system. Other scientists quickly embraced it and his fame spread. Linné was ennobled for his efforts and thus became entitled to a "von." This made him Carl von Linné, Latinized to read Carolus Linnaeus. Today his work is so well known that it is not always considered necessary to spell out his name entirely. You may see it as Linn. or simply as L. Except for Napoleon, I cannot think of another person who is universally known by a single initial.

In the system developed by Linnaeus, every living thing that has been studied and described has been given a name consisting of two or three words. This scientific name may be Latin or it may be a Greek word in Latin alphabet and grammar. The first word begins with a capital letter and it indicates the subject's

genus. The second word is always printed in lower case (even if it is derived from a person's name), and it tells us the *species.* The complete set of rules fills a book and requires the efforts of many people all over the world who are dedicated to the description and classification of living forms. Oh yes, the third word in a scientific name would be applied if a classifier believes that this organism, be it an elephant or a tree, was so closely related to another that it should be ranked as a subspecies.

The ideal situation arises when the first classification remains unchallenged. Then the name doesn't change. In point of fact,

this rarely happens. As we continue to learn about the nature of things, we gain new insights and new relationships are discovered. Also, sometimes old concepts of relationship are proven to be invalid. So, names are changed. For example, consider that the common eastern garter snake has been scientifically described eleven times! Linnaeus himself first did it in 1766. He called it *Coluber ordinatus.* Today we know it scientifically as *Thamnophis sirtalis sirtalis.* The other nine names are of interest only to specialist scientists. You can find them in the *Check List of North American Reptiles* by Karl P.

an interest in the other as well. Bird watchers rarely get involved with mollusks and mammologists are not frequently into fishes, but often a herpetologist will work on problems of both reptiles and amphibians. Herptile is often abbreviated to herp.

Classification

This section skims over a simplified, abridged, and less than perfect arrangment of the Tree of Life as it pertains to snakes. Don't be upset if you find another arrangement elsewhere that is not exactly the same as this one. Each reflects the opinions of scientists who, like you and me, are less than perfect. I'm absolutely certain, from the fossil record and other evidence, that all animals were not created at the same time, and also I am certain that their relationships are based on their evolution. I am also absolutely certain that no existing Tree of Life is completely and precisely flawless. What we do have is the best opinion of well-informed experts. Don't nit-pick what they offer and then throw out the baby with the bathwater. There is much to be learned from the Tree of Life even if some of its branches are presently a bit askew.

Schmidt. published by the American Society of Ichthyologists and Herpetologists, 1953. (Dr. Schmidt was later bitten in the thumb by a small African rear-fanged snake. He thought that his experience would be good to describe in a scientific journal, so he recorded his early symptoms and sensations. Sadly, the bite of this little snake proved to be fatal.)

Another useful word for you to know is herptile. A herptile is an amphibian *or* a reptile. They are often lumped under this name for convenience because the people who study either class often have

Start with that popular old aid to memory — King Philip Called Out For Good Soup, then use each initial letter to set up the Grand Scheme:

K - Kingdom
P - Phylum
C - Class
O - Order
F - Family
G - Genus
S - Species.

Now, in this Grand Scheme, our kingdom is Animalia, the animal kingdom. Here we set aside the plants and the fungi and some microbes. Next is the phylum, Chordata. This is where we take note of the notochord, a stiffener that runs the length of some primitive vertebrates. Not included in this phylum of chordates are the mollusks, worms, insects, spiders, crustaceans, and other "spineless" creatures. A snake is certainly a chordate. Other recognized systems of classification use words like Craniata and Vertebrata.

Class is the next category. Snakes are members of the class Reptilia, the reptiles. These are mostly "cold-blooded" animals with lungs but without hair or feathers. Some but not all are scaly. Included also are lizards, turtles, crocodilians, and tuataras, plus such fossils as the dinosaurs and plesiosaurs.

Order follows class, and now we look at the order Squamata, which consists of three suborders: lizards, amphisbaenians, and snakes. Lizards have eyelids (but do not necessarily have four legs or even two legs). Amphisbaenians are (usually) legless worm-like creatures that live underground. There are technical reasons why

lizards and amphisbaenians are not lumped. Snakes, then, are all alone in their own suborder, Serpentes. Here they comprise three superfamilies.

It is within these three groups that all snakes are systematically arranged. First are the Booidea; these are the "primitive" snakes, including pythons and boas and also several others not suitable for pet keepers. The next superfamily is the blindsnakes; by and large these are not kept as pets. Last, and most important for pet keepers, are the Colubroidea or advanced snakes. Most of our pets come either from this group or of course from the boas and pythons.

Let's look at this superfamily

The few living species of alligators, caimans, and crocodiles are not well-known to most people and few can be successfully kept in captivity for very long. Alligator mississippiensis.

Pelamis platurus, *one of the most widely distributed sea snakes. Sea snakes are now placed in Elapidae, but they were formerly given their own family, Hydrophiidae. Photo courtesy of R. E. Kuntz.*

you ever see that word "Ophidia" again, remember you saw it first right here. Is Serpentes an order or a suborder? Good question; it shows that you are thinking. Well, how about an answer? Oh yes, an answer — the answer is: It depends on who you ask.

Two more words, more useful than those in the last paragraph, are keeled (or carinated) and smooth. These words relate to the surface of the scales, especially on the snake's head and back. Belly scales are almost always quite smooth. Water snakes have keeled scales and racers are a good example of smooth scaled snakes.

Colubridea a bit more closely. Here we find the family Colubridae — note carefully the spelling — these words are not the same. These are the typical harmless snakes. There is plenty here to choose from for pet keeping.

The remaining two families in this superfamily Colubridea are:

Elapidae — the cobras and their relatives, all venomous. Shun them.

Viperidae — the adders and vipers, all venomous also. Shun them.

One structural feature of living snakes that is used by scientists to classify snakes into their family relationships is the male sexual organ. One problem arises: when a fossil of a snake is found, there is no part of this organ to study since it is not bony and hence it leaves no record in stone.

According to one recent and popular systematic arrangement, all snakes were placed in a suborder Ophidia. Today we place the snakes in Serpentes. If

One of the European vipers, Vipera berus. *The Viperidae now includes the pit vipers, once considered a full family, Crotalidae.*

Dr. Herndon G. Dowling is one of the best in this business of classification of reptiles, and here I take the liberty of quoting him from the 1974 *HISS Yearbook of Herpetology:*

"In any case it is clear that no one classification of reptiles is acceptable to all herpetologists, and that widely differing views are held by equally-competent taxonomists. A number of changes in both major and minor taxa are to be expected, therefore."

Glossary

This is a list of words that I have touched on only lightly or have totally avoided when writing this book. Many are unnecessary for successful snake keeping, but they often appear in the literature. So, against the time you read another book or wish to impress someone, here are a few technical words of herpetology.

Aestivation — See Estivation.

Albino — A lack of pigment in the skin. Pinkness is derived from the color of blood.

Anterior — Opposed to posterior. Anterior means front or close to the animal's head.

Anus — An opening at the base of the tail. See cloaca.

Arboreal — An animal that lives mostly in trees.

Cloaca — A single chamber which opens through the anus. The one chamber and one opening are utilized for both excretion and reproduction.

Crepuscular — Not necessarily active in broad daylight (diurnal) or at night (nocturnal), but rather more active at dawn, dusk, or twilight.

Cryptic — Concealing.

Diurnal — Active in broad daylight.

Dorsal — The back or upper

Probing the cloaca of a rat snake for the hemipenial pocket. This method of sexing captive snakes is now widely used but is still dangerous even with the proper tools. Probe kits are available from specialist suppliers. Photo by J. Gee.

part of the body of an animal.

Ecology — Biological economics, mutual relationships.

Ectotherm — Fishes, amphibians, mollusks, and of course reptiles are unable to do much to regulate their internal temperatures as would birds or mammals. Cold-blooded. The ectotherm therefore seeks the environment that provides the desired temperature.

Estivation — Akin to hibernation; a snake estivates when the climate is too dry and/or hot for comfort. It buries itself and remains dormant, thus conserving its body fluids until the weather improves. Also spelled aestivation.

Fossorial — It burrows or digs.

Gravid — A female bearing eggs or embryos.

Hemipenis — The copulatory organ of a male snake or lizard.

Herpetology — Scientific study of reptiles and amphibians.

Herptile — Amphibians and reptiles taken together.

Hibernation — Wintertime dormancy.

Hybrid — The result of mating unrelated parents (of different species). A mule is a hybrid resulting from the mating of a mare and a jackass.

Intergrade — Animals that seem to blend the characteristics of subspecies.

Jacobson's Organ — Organ for detecting odor. Located in roof of mouth. The tongue delivers the odor. The nostrils connect only with the lung or lungs.

Keel — A ridge on a scale.

Melanism — Blackness; opposite of albinism.

Neurotoxin — A poison that affects the nervous system.

Nocturnal — Active during the night.

Oviparous — The animal lays eggs, then later the eggs hatch.

Ovoviviparous—The animal holds its eggs inside its body until they hatch. Living young are delivered. See viviparous. Ovoviviparus means that the embryos are sustained by the contents of the egg and not by any connection to the mother.

Poikilothermal — A technical word for the variable temperature of cold-blooded animals.

Posterior — Toward the rear.

Prehensile tail — Capable of grasping or wrapping with the tail.

Subcaudals — Scales beneath the tail. Most snakes with subcaudals in a single row are venomous. Most with them in a double row are non-venomous. Don't count on it.

Terrestrial — An animal that lives on land.

Toxin — A poisonous substance.

Venom — A toxin produced by an animal.

Vent — Anus, the opening from the cloaca to the outside.

Ventral — The underside of a body.

Viviparous — Live-bearing animal whose young were nourished by a connection of some sort with the mother.

The common brown snake, Storeria dekayi, is a good example of a northern snake that hibernates during the winter and estivates during the dry summer. Photo by J. K. Langhammer.

Boas and Pythons

Native Boas

Boas and pythons are closely related, non-venomous constrictors. Pythons lay eggs and boas give birth to living young, but most scientists lump them all together in the same family (Boidae), regardless. Vestigial remnants of hind legs often appear as little spurs near the vent. There are only two native North American boa species.

The rubber boa, *Charina bottae*, grows to nearly 3 feet of desirable and attractive pet snake. It has a short blunt tail and a uniform color that can be reddish brown or tan or chocolate brown or even olive green. The spurs of the male are more prominent than those of the female. This snake swims well, burrows well, and climbs well. It is active at night. It is docile. It eats birds, mammals and lizards. It is found in Oregon south and east, south to California and even as far east as Montana and Colorado and also into British Columbia. Rubber boas have lived more than 11 years in captivity.

The rosy boa, *Lichanura trivirgata* and its several subspecies, is a desert snake that grows to a length of 3 ½ feet. It is relatively long-lived for a small snake — over 18 years has been recorded. Its habits are similar to those of the rubber boa, but its habitat is limited to southern California and nearby Arizona. Its colors vary with subspecies. Rosy boas are striped and/or speckled.

Exotic Boas and Pythons

Exotic simply means non-native or foreign. It doesn't necessarily mean tropical or even semi-tropical. Except for the native U.S. rubber boa and the rosy boa, all the boas and pythons are, for us, exotics. Of all the non-native snakes, the boas and pythons are surely the most desired by pet keepers and surely the most

Lichanura trivirgata, *the rosy boa, is one of only two boas native to the United States. Photo by K. Lucas, Steinhart Aqu.*

spectacular for exhibition. A 25-foot python is something a person is not likely to forget.

In 1975 I wrote a 96-page book entitled *All About Boas and Other Snakes,* also published by T.F.H., which listed the common and scientific names of about 40 of the better known boas and their natural distribution. Here is that list but now it is enlarged to about sixty, updated, and it reflects the changes of names which have, since then, been given to us by the classifiers. This list is in no way "official" or complete; it is here in this form to assist a novice snake keeper with names he probably never encountered before. For a more detailed coverage, consult *Pythons and Boas* by P.J. Stafford (T.F.H.)

The Kenyan sand boa, Eryx colubrinus loveridgei, *is one of the more commonly seen smaller boas. They are usually most at home in dry terraria, feeding on small rodents and lizards. Photo by P. J. Stafford.*

Abaco Island Boa; *Epicrates exsul* — Abaco, Bahamas
African Python or African Rock Python; *Python sebae* — Central and South Africa
Amazonian Tree Boa; *Corallus enydris eyndris* — Amazon River Basin
Amethystine Python; *Liasis (or Python) amethystinus* — Australia and New Guinea
Anaconda or Water Boa; *Eunectes murinus* — South America
Annulated Boa; *Corallus annulatus* — South America
Argentine Rainbow Boa; *Epicrates cenchria alvarezi* — Argentina, South America
Australian Python or Diamond Python; *Python spilotes* — Australia and New Guinea
Bahama Boa; *Epicrates striatus* — Southern Bahama Islands, Hispaniola

Exotic Boas and Pythons

Ball Python or Royal Python; *Python regius* — West Africa
Bimini Boa; *Epicrates striatus fosteri* — Bimini, Bahamas
Black-headed Python; *Aspidites melanocephalus* — Australia
Black-tailed Python or Indian Python; *Python molurus* — India, Sri Lanka, East Indies, China, Malay Peninsula, Java
Blood Python; *Python curtus* — Indo-China to Borneo and Sumatra
Boa Constrictor; *Boa constrictor* — South America north into Mexico
Brown Sand Boa, Indian Sand Boa, or Two-Headed Snake; *Eryx johni* — India
Burmese Python; *Python molurus bivittatus* — Burma
Calabar Burrowing Python; *Calabaria reinhardti* — West Africa
Carpet Python; *Python spilotes* — Australia and New Guinea
Central American Boa; *Boa constrictor* — Southern Mexico to South America
Ceylonese Python; *Python molurus pimbura* — Sri Lanka (Ceylon)
Colombian Rainbow Boa; *Epicrates cenchria maurus* — Colombia, South America
Colombian Boa; *Boa constrictor* — Colombia, South America
Cook's Tree Boa or Tree Boa; *Corallus enydris cooki* — South America, Lesser Antilles
Cuban Boa; *Epicrates angulifer* — Cuba
D'Albert's Python; *Liasis albertisi* — New Guinea
Diamond Python or Australian Python; *Python spilotes* — Australia, New Guinea

The common boa constrictor is actually called Boa constrictor. *It is certainly the most commonly sold boa in the United States and perhaps the one most likely to survive in the hands of the beginner. If properly cared for and well-fed, there is no reason why captive boas should not regularly mate in captivity. Photo by B. Kahl.*

Dumeril's Boa; *Acrantophis dumerili* — Madagascar
Emerald Boa or Green Tree Boa; *Corallus caninus* — South America
Egyptian Sand Boa or Sand Boa; *Eryx jaculus* — North Africa, Ionian Islands, Greece, Southwest and Central Asia
Green Python; *Chondropython viridis* — New Guinea and northern Australia
Green Tree Boa or Emerald Boa; *Corallus caninus* — South America
Guyanan Rainbow Boa; *Epicrates cenchria* — Guyana, South America
Haitian Boa; *Epicrates striatus striatus* — Hispaniola
Haitian Dwarf Boa; *Tropidophis haetianus* — Hispaniola
Haitian Rock Boa; *Epicrates fordi* — Hispaniola
Haitian Vine Boa; *Epicrates gracilis* — Hispaniola
Indian Python or Black-tailed Python; *Python molurus* — India, Sri Lanka (Ceylon), East Indies, China, Malay Peninsula, Java
Indian Sand Boa; *Eryx johni* — India
Kenyan Sand Boa; *Eryx colubrinus loveridgei* — Kenya
Madagascar Tree Boa; *Sanzinia madagascariensis* — Madagascar
Malayan Python; *Python curtus* — Indo-China to Borneo and Sumatra
Mexican Boa; *Boa constrictor imperator* — Mexico, Central America to South America
Peruvian Red-tailed Boa; *Boa constrictor* — Peru, S. A.
Rainbow Boa; *Epicrates cenchria* — Central to South America
Reticulated Python or Regal Python; *Python reticulatus* — S.E. Asia, East Indies
Rosy Boa; *Lichanura trivirgata* — Southwest U.S. and adjacent Mexico
Rough-scaled Sand Boa; *Gongylophis* or *Eryx conicus* — India, Pakistan, Sri Lanka
Royal Python; *Python regius* — West Africa
Rubber Boa; *Charina bottae* — Western North America
Sand Boa or Egyptian Sand Boa; *Eryx jaculus* — Asia, Algeria, S.E. Europe, Egypt
Solomon Islands Ground Boa; *Candoia candoia* — Solomon Islands
Red Tailed Boa; *Acrantophis dumerili* — Madagascar
Tree Boa or Cook's Tree Boa; *Corallus endyris* — South America, Lesser Antilles
Turk's Island Boa; *Epicrates chrysogaster* — Bahamas
Two-Headed Snake or Indian Sand Boa or Brown Sand Boa; *Eryx johni* — India
Water Boa or Anaconda; *Eunectes murinus* — South America
West Indian Boa; *Boa constrictor orophias* — Lesser Antilles
Yellow Anaconda; *Eunectes notaeus* — Central South America
Yellow Tree Boa; *Corallus enydris cooki* — Tropical South America, Lesser Antilles

Now that you have seen the list you may wonder which species you would like to own. Your finances will perhaps crimp your style, but more importantly, you should consider disposition and size before making your choice. Here is a brief rundown on a few of the more readily available snakes in this group.

Anaconda — Reputed to grow to 30 feet, which would make it one of the world's longest snakes. These snakes are easily fed in captivity and they live a long time, but many like to spend long periods immersed in water, so they are difficult to display. Some fanciers keep them in dry cages and they do remain healthy. Anacondas are not as easily tamed as boa constrictors, and many are plain mean.

Boa Constrictor — Smaller than an anaconda, this snake is considered by many to be one of the most beautiful of the family. It is most desirable because it is readily tamed and easy to maintain.

Mexican Boa — This name is applied to almost any boa constrictor from Mexico or Central America. They are popular pets. A Mexican boa can be kept in a 50-gallon aquarium or a cage of that approximate size. Mexican boas might be a bit less easy to tame than South American boa constrictors, but nevertheless they are very popular pets.

Sand Boas — Resemble our native rubber boas. They are small, blunt-tailed, gentle, and hardy. Regrettably, they like to burrow in sand and so are not good for display.

Cuban Boas and various Tree Boas — They are difficult or even impossible to tame. They are not recommended for a beginner.

African Rock Python — Will grow to an average length of 16 feet. This is a hardy snake and it can be tamed successfully.

Indian Pythons — Though mean when wild, most are easily tamed. There are several types and all are popular with zoo keepers, circuses, and pet snake owners.

Rainbow Boas — This is a popular exotic species for pet keepers. It is available in or through pet shops and is a good beginner's pet. In my home town Christopher Trecker, who was then about 11 years old, was given a rainbow boa by his parents. It was then about 3 feet long and hardly thicker than my thumb. Chris fed it on mice and it grew slowly. In four years it gained about a foot and a half and trebled its girth. It ate one mouse every two weeks. The Trecker family considered it to be a good pet and now, as an upper classman in college, Chris is considering getting another snake. I would guess that his rainbow boa could have grown a good deal more and faster if it had been fed more generously.

Although Australia has several spectacular pythons, most are not available with any regularity on the market. The yellow-headed Ramsay's python, Aspidites ramsayi, *is no exception. Photo by R. T. Hoser.*

Popular Native Pet Species

My first pet snake was a garter that I caught when I found it hiding under a scrap of rusty sheet metal in an open field. It bit me and then it smelled something terrible when it defecated on my clothes, but within a few days I had it docile and eating earthworms out of my hand. As a boy I never owned an exotic variety; all were native species that I caught or got from my friends. These included rat snakes, water snakes, ringnecks, snake or two, but kingsnakes, pine snakes, and some other larger types are now often illegal in some areas. Check before you get that snake — you don't want to get into trouble with the law.

Racers

Whipsnakes and racers are high-speed animals but not necessarily bent on escape. Some will attack if cornered and others will ignore a person if encountered. In a bare cage a racer will be nervous and

green snakes, hognoses, milk snakes, more garters, ribbon snakes, and a worm snake that I soon released because it would never show itself. A great variety of common and keepable snakes certainly grace our country. Remember though, that in many states the type of species you can collect and keep is regulated by law. Probably no one will care if you take a water snake or garter

Most hobbyists consider the racers and whipsnakes to be too nervous to make good pets. Masticophis lateralis. *Photo by J. Dodd.*

excited. It will not eat and its snout will be rubbed raw from striking the cage walls and attempting to escape. Put some natural hiding places and a small upturned box into a roomy cage

74

Expensive boas and pythons are often housed in expensive cages. This baby emerald boa has plenty of room to grow up in.

and your racer will settle down beautifully and might well become a great pet.

Whipsnakes (genus *Masticophis*) and racers (genus *Coluber*) grow to considerable lengths — a coachwhip could grow to a length of 8 feet.

These snakes do nicely on dead mice, and they will also eat other snakes if the opportunity arises. Their quarters must be kept bone dry or skin diseases will result. They do drink water from a bowl or dish, but the cage bottom of sand, earth, or wood chips must be kept bone dry.

Water Snakes

By and large, native water snakes do not make good pets. One reason is that they do best if they can spend a good deal of their time immersed in water. Their cage needs to be at least partially an aquarium, and it will certainly require a great deal of effort by you to keep the water from fouling. No conventional aquarium pump-filter arrangement will suffice, as the snake will escape through or around it. The snake will plug-up or break the plumbing. The filter will not be adequate for the volume of debris that the snake generates. After you have out-smarted me and your captive by building a foolproof filter system, what exactly will you have accomplished? You will then have living accommodations for a genus of snakes, *Nerodia*

you will see that there is but a single row of scales on the underside of the tail, but a non-venomous water snake has a double row (you might say two rows or you might say that these scales are divided) from the vent to the tip of the tail. (All venomous North American pit vipers have undivided scales from the vent to the tail tip on the underside, but at least one of our non-venomous snakes is also that way. This exception is the long-nose snake (*Rhinocheilus*) of the Southwest. It doesn't have an especially long nose. It is nocturnal and secretive and makes a poor captive pet.)

Water snakes produce soft

(formerly *Natrix*), that are prone to bite even the hand that feeds them. They fight with great spirit and rarely become docile in captivity.

Water snakes grow to a length of 6 feet (but many are smaller) and give birth to living young. They eat crayfish, fish, frogs, tadpoles, and salamanders. Some species of water snakes resemble the venomous cottonmouth moccasin, which also favors a watery habitat. If you examine a very dead cottonmouth moccasin

Although its color pattern is striking, the longnose snake is considered to do too poorly in captivity to be kept by most hobbyists. They seldom feed well on even the juiciest lizards and mice. Rhinocheilus lecontei. Photo by J. K. Langhammer.

smelly and watery feces that make quite a mess in the cage or aquarium. This is still another drawback to keeping them as captive pets.

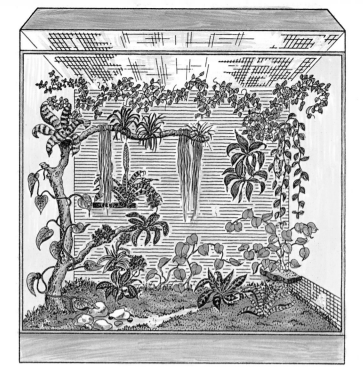

Although these fancy terraria may look great to the keeper, they are just not suitable for keeping most snakes. In the first place, anything but a large arboreal boa or python would immediately disappear into the shrubbery never to be seen again. The plants would have to be replaced frequently. But the major problem is—how do you clean out a cage this complicated?

Garter Snakes

There are about 50 species and subspecies of garter snakes in the lower 48 states. Most are common, easy to catch, and easy to maintain. Some favor mountain areas and others spend so much of their time in water that we might call them water snakes. The largest individual of the largest variety might be all of 4 feet long, but most are a great deal smaller. The young are born alive in litters of as many as a hundred and as miniatures of their parents are all of 6 inches long and ready to eat worms.

When you catch a garter snake it will try to wrap itself around your arm and it will discharge some awful smelling matter from its cloaca. This is your initiation to snake catching, but fortunately a garter is easily tamed and a tame garter snake is virtually odorless.

A garter snake is sexually mature by its third year and a normal life expectancy might be ten or 12 years. If you keep your pet in a frost-free environment you can expect it to eat a couple of worms a day or a small frog or a small fish every few days. If you feed it less quantity or less frequently it will still survive, but it will not grow as rapidly or as large as it might otherwise.

Garters are in the genus *Thamnophis,* which also includes the ribbon snakes. These latter tend to be more slender, faster moving, and somewhat more nervous than most of the snakes we commonly call garters.

Hognose Snakes

This is an interesting and much misunderstood snake. No one ever said it was beautiful, but it does make a good pet. The hognose is an expert at feigning death. It is also an expert at bluffing about its ability to defeat

The western hognose snake makes a fairly good pet as it has less of a tendency to feed exclusively on toads, taking an occasional lizard or frog. Heterodon nasicus. *Photo by K. Lucas, Steinhart Aqu.*

Ribbon snakes are much like garter snakes in every respect except they sometimes tend to be a bit more aquatic. Thamnophis proximus. *Photo by J. K. Langhammer.*

its enemies. When it fails at the latter ploy it resorts to the former. Many people have been fooled by a "dead" hognose that silently disappeared, and others were equally fooled by this harmless snake that behaved as though it had enough venom to wipe out the entire Democratic Party. When a hognose coils and spreads its jaws and hisses, it looks like a cottonmouth or copperhead ready to explode.

The hognose is a tough snake. I have seen them swimming across tidal creeks several hundred feet

wide in search of new hunting grounds. I have also seen one in near-freezing weather poking around in holes where a frog or a toad might be hiding.

The hognose will avidly eat toads that would sicken a dog. It will actually seek them out as an article of diet. It subdues its prey with a slightly venomous saliva that also seems to lubricate the prey and help it slide down the snake's gullet.

A hognose could be one of three species in the genus *Heterodon*. There are, conveniently, a western, an eastern, and a southern species. There are no hognose snakes in the Western Rockies or in the Pacific Coast states. Their habits and general appearance are about the same. The female lays as many as two dozen eggs in sand or soft loam. Each is about an inch and a quarter long. They hatch in two months and are mature in two years. A really large eastern hognose might be 4 feet long; the other species are smaller.

Indigo Snakes

This single species, *Drymarchon corais,* comes in several subspecies, but in our area it only occurs in southern Texas, Florida, and states near Florida. This is a highly desirable large snake, so much so that some varieties were legally protected in many places. Indigos of all the various subspecies (Mexican and Central American forms are still available) must be kept warm and dry. They will eat anything that they can get around, be it mouse, rat, bird, fish, amphibian, lizard, or even another snake. They lay eggs and have been bred in captivity. This snake must not be caged with other snakes of any size, shape, or species.

Rat Snakes and Corn Snakes

There are a considerable number of species and subspecies ranging in length to 6 feet. All are in the genus *Elaphe,* and although some look superficially like the copperhead, all are perfectly non-venomous. Among this genus are some of the most beautiful snakes in North America. They do well in captivity and usually become tame in a short time. A great deal of the taming of a snake depends on how you act and how you establish the furnishings of the cage. Is it the correct size? Roomy enough for a hiding place? Is the bottom dry and clean? Is there clean, fresh drinking water always available? Is the temperature adequate —

Eastern indigo snake and her eggs. Drymarchon corais couperi. Photo by J. Gee.

ranging between 65° and 75°F.?

Some types of rat snakes are a solid black and others are yellow with dark stripes and still others are blotched; still another from the Everglades of Florida is a large bright orange animal. Spectacular!

Kingsnakes

Some snakes poison their prey and then eat it. Others simply sneak up, grab, and swallow. Still others subdue their victims by wrapping coils of their bodies around the unfortunate one and thus prevent it from breathing. Such behavior causes us to call them constrictors. They don't thoroughly crush their prey — no bones are broken. Death comes primarily by suffocation. There is some evidence (or at least speculation) that a rabbit locked in a snake's embrace might die of fright even before it suffocated.

So then, if a snake wraps itself around its victim and squeezes, we call it a constrictor. The pythons and boas are all recognized as constrictors of course, but there are still others, unrelated by virtue of their anatomy but nevertheless constrictors. All these latter are also non-venomous. The kingsnakes are the best known in this group, and the common kingsnake, *Lampropeltis getulus,* is the species to look at first. There are some eight subspecies that together cover the U.S.A. from southern New Jersey to Florida and west across the southern states to California and southwestern Oregon, then south into Mexico. Some are found in pine barrens and others in fields, prairie, chaparral, desert, and swamp — truly a snake for many temperate climes. Kingsnakes lay as many as two dozen eggs that hatch in about ten weeks,

A beautifully marked milk snake or tricolored kingsnake, Lampropeltis triangulum annulata, *from northern Mexico. The many subspecies of tricolored kings are exceedingly desirable pets but some are protected by law. Photo by K. Lucas, Steinhart Aqu.*

depending on the temperature. Nearly a foot long when they hatch, these kingsnakes commonly grow to a length of 5 feet and may reach nearly 7 feet. Most are black or partly black with white, yellow, or tan markings.

Kingsnakes eat lizards, birds, mice, eggs, and other snakes, including *all* our native venomous snakes! Kingsnakes seem to be at least partially immune to snake venom.

The genus *Lampropeltis* includes several other well known and desirable species, and some are protected by law because of their scarcity. The scarlet kingsnake is especially well known because it is so beautiful and also because it superficially resembles the deadly coral snake. It is a type of milk snake. There are several similar banded kingsnakes (milk snakes actually) that are called tricolored kings —

all are expensive and most are regulated by law.

Snakes with ring patterns of red, yellow (or white), and black are either perfectly harmless (milk snakes, scarlet snakes, etc.) or extremely dangerous (coral snakes). There is a quick recognition guide to be found in the *arrangement* of the colored rings. Here is a ditty to help you to remember which is which for *North American* ringed snakes:

Red to black, venom lack.
Red to yellow, kill a fellow.

If a red ring butts up against a yellow ring, you may be looking at a deadly coral snake whose poison could easily be more toxic than that of a cobra. Its head need not be triangular in order to be venomous. The head shape is meaningless when it comes to measuring danger.

Note: This ditty is applicable only to North American native snakes. There are South American coral snakes whose patterns do *not* fit this rule. In nature, rules are broken constantly. Remember, Mother Nature didn't make the rules; we did, and we are not perfect.

So, then, in the U.S.A. this red to yellow rule will surely protect you, but it also includes two snakes that are quite harmless. These are the shovel-nosed snakes, genus *Chionactis*. Both do have a red-to-yellow pattern, but they are not banded much like milk snakes or coral snakes. Both are non-venomous.

Many harmless snakes are needlessly killed by well-meaning

No, this is not another tricolored kingsnake. It is a slightly aberrant (too much white) specimen of the venomous Arizona coral snake, Micruroides euryxanthus. *Photo by Dr. S. A. Minton.*

Gopher snakes are considered excellent pets if you like larger snakes. This individual belongs to a striped phase of the common Pituophis melanoleucus catenifer. Photo by K. Lucas, Steinhart Aqu.

but ignorant people who feel it is their duty to exterminate every serpent. This is to be regretted, especially since so many snakes eat mice and rats that do much harm by destroying food and spreading disease.

Bull and Pine Snakes

The bull snake is a constrictor relative of the kingsnakes. Bull snakes grow to a length of 9 feet, (more commonly 6 to 7 feet), are popular in circuses, and are great at eating rodents. There are three (more or less) species that are organized into ten (more or less) subspecies. The pine snake, *Pituophis melanoleucus,* is found in the southeast and Gulf states. Bull snakes (*P. sayi*) are found in the midwest, and the western form is called a gopher snake (*P.*

catenifer). Together these three cover most of the lower 48 except for New York and New England. Don't get carried away with their scientific names, just enjoy them as pets — many herpetologists today lump every *Pituophis* into one species, *P. melanoleucas.*

Small bull snakes, pine snakes, and gopher snakes eat mice.

Although beautiful to look at, ringneck snakes seldom make good pets. They tend to be secretive and sometimes very specific in their food requirements. Specimens from the northeastern U. S. often require salamanders as part of the diet. Diadophis punctatus. *Photo by K. Lucas, Steinhart Aqu.*

Larger specimens will work their way up to rabbits.

Mud Snake and Rainbow Snake

Once these snakes were in separate genera, but they are now placed in the same genus. That is to say we, the people, have decided that they, the snakes, are now in the same genus. To feed one, John F. Breen advises us to keep a siren or an amphiuma in the freezer. Then, to feed one of these 4-foot beauties you would rub a frog over that frozen salamander until it smelled like a salamander. Then the snake would eat the frog. If you do it right, your pet could thrive in captivity for 18 years. But would

Ringneck Snake

the salamander last that long in the freezer?

Each species has a spine in the tip of its tail, leading to the belief by many that the spine is a "stinger" with a powerful poison.

Farancia erytrogramma, the rainbow snake, eats eels without any salamander rubdown. This creature has been dubbed "hoop snake," "thunderbolt," and "stinging snake" as a result of some absurd myths.

Farancia abacura, the mud snake, lays as many as 100 eggs, and the female may "incubate" them until they hatch — maybe eight weeks later. This snake is native to the southeastern coast, Florida, the lower Mississippi Valley, and the Gulf coast.

Green Snakes
There are two native green snakes, a northern form that is commonly known as the smooth green snake, *Opheodrys vernalis,* and grows to a foot and a half in length; and a southern form, the keeled or rough green snake,

Opheodrys aestivus, which reaches 3 feet. These two species are slender, gentle, and lovely to look at. They lay eggs. The young are dark at first, but become green as they mature.

These snakes will eat crickets, spiders and hairless caterpillars. It is hard to maintain these species in captivity, probably because we don't fully understand their natural diet.

Ringneck Snake
Or shall we say ringneck snakes? The latest opinion is that there is but one species separated into a number of subspecies. None exceed 3 feet, most are less than 2 feet, and those from the East tend to be even smaller. This or these are *Diadophis punctatus.* They eat still smaller snakes, salamanders, and earthworms. You should keep them in a planted terrarium with plenty of hiding places. Every one I have ever caught had been hiding under a rock.

Above: *A green snake is a green snake is a green snake. This Asian species,* Opheodrys (or Liopeltis) major, *looks just like the American* O. vernalis. *Photo courtesy R. E. Kuntz.*

Right: *The corn snake,* Elaphe guttata, *is perhaps currently the most popular North American snake in captivity. Large numbers are bred for sale, including various color phases. Photo by M. Gilroy.*

Next

It is impossible to show and describe all of the U.S. snakes suitable for snake keepers in this book. There are approximately 250 native U.S. varieties, and a good percentage make satisfactory pets. Don't be troubled by that word "approximately"; the number of species is pretty well fixed, but the opinions of the experts are subject to change regarding the status of species and especially subspecies.

There are several good books to help you with the identification of the native U.S. snakes. Try these:

A Field Guide to Reptiles and

Amphibians of the U.S. and Canada East of the 100th Meridian by Conant. Published by Houghton Mifflin, Boston.

A companion to the above by Stebbins is what you should be using if you are going to meet up with any western snakes.

Reptiles and Amphibians by Zim and Smith. Published by the Golden Press, New York.

The Audubon Society Field Guide to North American Reptiles and Amphibians by Behler and King. Published by A. A. Knopf, New York.

The next thing you might do as your interest builds up would be to join a local or national herpetological society. If you are also interested in fishes, you might join the American Society of Ichthyologists and Herpetologists. Their most recent address will always be available by writing to the Division of Reptiles, National Museum of Natural History (Smithsonian Institution), Washington, D. C. 20560. This is the organization that publishes *Copeia,* a quarterly journal. *Copeia* was named to honor Edward Drinker Cope (1840-1897). In 1875 Cope came out with his *Check-List of North American Batrachia and Reptilia,* and in 1913 John Treadwell Nichols founded the Society and named the journal to honor Cope. When I was a boy, I met Nichols; he was one of my heroes.

In 1936 the journal *Herpetologica* was first published. It is under the banner of the Herpetologists' League and its

Typhlops braminus, the first snake to be accidentally established in the United States. This small burrower reproduces by virgin birth (parthenogenesis). Photo courtesy R. E. Kuntz.

most recent address can always be obtained by writing to the U. S. National Museum.

The Society for the Study of Amphibians and Reptiles (SSAR) publishes a journal and also Reviews and Circulars. SSAR invites anyone who is interested to join. To reach them, write to the Department of Zoology, Miami aforementioned major societies (especially SSAR). If you still have trouble finding a nearby herpetologists' society or snake fanciers' association or whatever, and your local pet dealer is unable to help, you might call the reptile department of your nearest zoo or natural history museum. Another route to follow

The checkered garter snake, Thamnophis marcianus. *Photo by K. Lucas, Steinhart Aqu.*

University of Ohio, Oxford, Ohio 45056.

There are many local organizations you might become interested in. To find them, start with a letter to one of the is through the zoology department of any nearby college.

So now I've told you what I was going to tell you: Start slowly; shun venomous species; be observant; gain experience; handle and house your animals humanely; and if you want to make money, *real money,* stay out of the snake business.

Suggested Reading

Diseases of Reptiles
Dr. H.-H. Reichenbach-Klinke and
E. Elkan
ISBN 0-87666-045-6
TFH PS-207
660 pages; 76 B & W photos
An essential reference for the
advanced hobbyist trying to learn
more about the diseases and
parasites of wild and captive
reptiles, including snakes.
Technical.

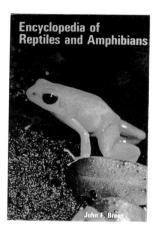

Beginning With Snakes
Richard F. Stratton
ISBN 0-87666-934-8
TFH KW-127
96 pages; 52 color photos; 22
B & W photos
Basic introduction to snake care.
Non-technical.

The T.F.H. Book of Snakes
Thomas Leetz
ISBN 0-87666-561-X
TFH HP-017
96 pages; 95 color photos
Lavishly illustrated large-format
book on natural history of snakes,
with good sections on sexing and
breeding. Non-technical.

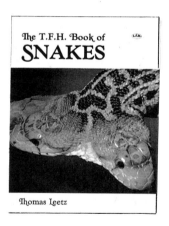

Encyclopedia of Reptiles and Amphibians
John F. Breen
ISBN 0-87666-220-3
TFH H-935
576 pages; 267 color photos; 316
B & W photos
Fine introduction to the world of
living herps. Covers both native
and exotic snakes in detail, with
information on natural history of
most species commonly kept in
captivity. Section on feeding live
foods. Non-technical.

Breeding Terrarium Animals
Elke Zimmermann
ISBN 0-86622-182-4
TFH H-1078
384 pages; 175 color photos;
numerous line drawings
The best book available on
captive breeding of herps, including
commonly kept snake species,
both native and exotic. Must
reading for the serious hobbyist.
Moderately technical.

Snakes of South America
Dr. Marcos A. Freiberg
ISBN 0-87666-912-7
TFH PS-758
160 pages; 111 color photos; 20
B & W photos

One of the few books available on the snake fauna of South America. Includes photos of many species, key to genera, checklist, identification drawings, natural history notes on common and interesting species, large bibliography. Technical.

Snakes as Pets
Dr. Hobart M. Smith
ISBN 0-87666-908-9
TFH AP-925
160 pages; 51 color photos; 55
B & W photos

A standard reference by a prominent American herpetologist on collecting and keeping North American snakes as pets; heavily illustrated, with many western species. Non-technical.

Pythons and Boas
Peter J. Stafford
ISBN 0-86622-183-2
TFH PS-846
192 pages; 111 color photos; 22
B & W photos plus numerous line drawings

The best coverage of the popular pythons and boas. Must reading for every hobbyist with even a passing interest in the group. Excellent natural history and care sections, with many species (common and uncommon) illustrated in color. Moderately technical.

Boas and Other Non-venomous Snakes
Werner Frank
ISBN 0-87666-922-4
TFH KW-002
96 pages; 27 color photos; 53
B & W photos

Good introduction to captive snakes, with emphasis on diseases and easy to keep species. Non-technical.

The World of Venomous Animals
Dr. Marcos Freiberg and Jerry G. Walls
ISBN 0-87666-567-9
TFH H-1068
192 pages; 282 color photos

Not strictly on snakes, but on all groups of venomous animals.

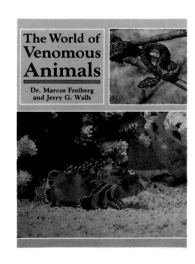

Index

Snakes must eat too. If the sight of a
snake constricting a small rodent is
repulsive to you, it would be best if
you do not consider snakes as a
hobby.

CO-023

A COMPLETE INTRODUCTION TO

SNAKES

COMPLETELY ILLUSTRATED IN FULL COLOR

The spectacular colors of this milk snake, Lampropeltis triangulum, *have made it a very popular species with advanced hobbyists.*